Cooking Light

soups
& stews
tonight!

Cooking Light

soups
& stews
tonight!

Oxmoor House®

ISBN-13: 978-0-8487-3360-5
ISBN-10: 0-8487-3360-6
Library of Congress Control Number: 2011931613

Printed in the United States of America
Second Printing 2012

Be sure to check with your health-care provider before making any changes in your diet.

Oxmoor House
VP, Publishing Director: Jim Childs
Editorial Director: Susan Payne Dobbs
Brand Manager: Michelle Turner Aycock
Senior Editor: Heather Averett
Managing Editor: Laurie S. Herr

Cooking Light® Soups & Stews Tonight!
Editor: Shaun Chavis
Project Editors: Sarah H. Doss, Holly D. Smith
Assistant Designer: Allison Sperando Potter
Director, Test Kitchens: Elizabeth Tyler Austin
Assistant Directors, Test Kitchens: Julie Christopher, Julie Gunter
Test Kitchens Professionals: Wendy Ball, R.D.; Allison E. Cox; Victoria E. Cox; Margaret Monroe Dickey; Alyson Moreland Haynes; Stefanie Maloney; Callie Nash; Catherine Crowell Steele; Leah Van Deren
Photography Director: Jim Bathie
Senior Photo Stylist: Kay E. Clarke
Associate Photo Stylist: Katherine Eckert Coyne
Assistant Photo Stylist: Mary Louise Menendez
Production Manager: Theresa Beste-Farley

Contributors
Copy Editor: Adrienne Davis
Proofreader: Jacqueline Giovanelli
Indexer: Nanette Cardon
Interns: Erin Bishop, Maribeth Browning, Blair Gillespie, Laura Hoxworth, Alison Loughman, Lindsay A. Rozier

Time Home Entertainment, Inc.
Publisher: Richard Fraiman
VP, Strategy & Business Development: Steven Sandonato
Executive Director, Marketing Services: Carol Pittard
Executive Director, Retail & Special Sales: Tom Mifsud
Director, New Product Development: Peter Harper
Director, Bookazine Development & Marketing: Laura Adam
Assistant Director, Brand Marketing: Joy Butts
Associate Counsel: Helen Wan

Cooking Light®
Editor: Scott Mowbray
Creative Director: Carla Frank
Deputy Editor: Phillip Rhodes
Executive Editor, Food: Ann Taylor Pittman
Special Publications Editor: Mary Simpson Creel, MS, RD
Senior Food Editor: Julianna Grimes
Senior Editor: Cindy Hatcher
Associate Food Editor: Timothy Q. Cebula
Assistant Editor, Nutrition: Sidney Fry, MS, RD
Assistant Editors: Kimberly Holland, Phoebe Wu
Test Kitchen Director: Vanessa T. Pruett
Assistant Test Kitchen Director: Tiffany Vickers Davis
Recipe Testers and Developers: Robin Bashinsky, Adam Hickman, Deb Wise
Art Director: Fernande Bondarenko
Junior Deputy Art Director: Alexander Spacher
Associate Art Director: Rachel Lasserre
Designer: Chase Turberville
Photo Director: Kristen Schaefer
Assistant Photo Editor: Amy Delaune
Senior Photographer: Randy Mayor
Senior Photo Stylist: Cindy Barr
Photo Stylist: Leigh Ann Ross
Chief Food Stylist: Charlotte Autry
Senior Food Stylist: Kellie Gerber Kelley
Copy Chief: Maria Parker Hopkins
Assistant Copy Chief: Susan Roberts
Research Editor: Michelle Gibson Daniels
Editorial Production Director: Liz Rhoades
Production Editor: Hazel R. Eddins
Assistant Production Editor: Josh Rutledge
Administrative Coordinator: Carol D. Johnson
Cookinglight.com Editor: Allison Long Lowery
Nutrition Editor: Holley Johnson Grainger, MS, RD
Production Assistant: Mallory Daugherty

To order additional publications, call 1–800–765–6400 or 1-800-491-0551.

For more books to enrich your life, visit **oxmoorhouse.com**

To search, savor, and share thousands of recipes, visit **myrecipes.com**

Cover: All-American Chili, page 160
Back cover (clockwise from top left): Broccoli and Chicken Noodle Soup, page 36; Chunky Vegetarian Chili, page 145; Loaded Potato Soup, page 65; Cioppino-Style Seafood Stew, page 109; Cincinnati Turkey Chili, page 151; Carrot-Parsnip Soup with Parsnip Chips, page 205

introduction

There's no better comfort food than a warm bowl of soup, stew, or chili. A bowl of soup can chase away colds or take you around the world with interesting, flavorful ingredients. And what's game night without chili? Soups, stews, and chilis make convenient weeknight dinners, too—they're perfect for make-ahead meals and many make great one-dish meals.

We—the editors of *Cooking Light* magazine—put together this collection of 140 of our favorite soup, stew, and chili recipes. These are the foods we like to fill our bowls with. You'll find plenty of classics, like the **All-American Chili** on the cover (page 160); **Quick Chicken Noodle Soup** (page 33) that is worthy of being part of your family's repertoire; **Simple Clam Chowder** (page 193); and **Tomato-Basil Soup** (page 20) that's ideal for pairing with a grilled cheese sandwich. We also included vegetarian soups like **Black Bean Soup** (page 59) and **Butternut Squash Soup with Spiced Seeds** (page 207). We couldn't forget favorites with international flavors, such as **Pasta e Fagioli** (page 31), **Fiery Tofu and Coconut Curry Soup** (page 68), and **Chipotle Chicken Tortilla Soup** (page 81). Flip through the pages to find some refreshing cold soups for hot summer days and a chapter of bread and salad recipes to round out your meals.

This book offers you more than just a collection of recipes: Our **Cooking Class** chapter (page 8) shows you how to make homemade stock from scratch and offers great tips on how to freeze soups and stews for later. With how-to photos and step-by-step techniques, you'll master the basics with ease.

With *Cooking Light Soups & Stews Tonight!,* our dedicated staff of culinary professionals and registered dietitians gives you all the tools and recipes you'll need to prepare healthful, delicious soups, stews, chilis, and chowders any night of the week. Let these kitchen-tested recipes breathe new life into the idea of having *Soups & Stews Tonight!*

The *Cooking Light* Editors

contents

cooking class

Soup is the true melting pot of all the world's best ingredients. And at *Cooking Light*, we've found that soup can be one of the best introductions to the genius and chemistry of cooking.

All About Soup

Soup is basic. Its techniques are classic. And by blending time-honored skills such as sautéing, caramelizing, deglazing, and thickening, you can have a meal on the table without feeling overwhelmed or intimidated. Just remember, it all starts with the stock or broth.

Stocks: The key to a great soup is a homemade stock. The slow simmering of meats, vegetables, herbs, and spices produces a flavorful liquid—the foundation for soup. Making homemade stock creates an intense natural flavor while keeping the amount of sodium low.

Broths: A broth is basically made from the same ingredients as a stock. However, broth is cooked in less time, isn't as intensely flavored, and often contains more sodium. Broths may be used in place of stock when you are short on time.

Commercial Products: Homemade stocks and broths are superior to commercial products, but they're not always practical. In those cases, we suggest using commercial products.

Stock Versus Broth Nutritional Comparisons

Here's how homemade and commercial stocks and broths compare nutritionally:

Ingredient (1 cup)	Calories	Fat	Sodium
Homemade beef stock	8	0.3g	9mg
Regular commercial beef stock	15	1g	890mg
*Fat-free, lower-sodium beef broth	15	1g	440mg
Homemade white chicken stock	28	0.8g	18mg
Regular commercial chicken stock	10	0.5g	960mg
*Fat-free, lower-sodium chicken broth	15	0g	570mg
Homemade vegetable stock	8	0.1g	2mg
*Lower-sodium organic vegetable broth	15	0g	570mg

Cooking Light Test Kitchens prefer to use Swanson's Natural Goodness Chicken Broth and Emeril's All Natural Organic Vegetable Stock in recipes.

Essential Techniques for Making Stocks

Master the art of making stocks with this step-by-step guide.

White Chicken Stock

White stock is best to use when you need a mild flavor that won't overpower delicate ingredients, and it's also good to keep in the freezer for other recipes. Its light color suits risotto, mashed potatoes, and cream soups. White stock is prepared entirely on the stovetop.

Yield: 10 cups (serving size: 1 cup)

½ teaspoon black peppercorns

10 parsley sprigs

8 thyme sprigs

3 celery stalks, cut into 2-inch-thick pieces

3 bay leaves

2 medium onions, peeled and quartered

2 carrots, cut into 2-inch-thick pieces

2 garlic cloves, crushed

6 pounds chicken pieces

16 cups cold water

1. Place first 8 ingredients in an 8-quart stockpot; add chicken and water. Bring mixture to a boil over medium heat. Reduce heat, and simmer, uncovered, 3 hours, skimming surface occasionally to remove foam. Strain stock through a fine sieve into a large bowl. Reserve chicken for another use; discard remaining solids. Cool stock to room temperature, then cover and chill stock 8 hours. Skim solidified fat from surface of stock; discard fat. Refrigerate stock in an airtight container for up to 1 week, or freeze for up to 3 months.

Calories 28; Fat 0.8g (sat 0.2g, mono 0.3g, poly 0.2g); Protein 4.7g; Carb 0.4g; Fiber 0.1g; Chol 15mg; Iron 0.3mg; Sodium 18mg; Calc 4mg

How to Make White Chicken Stock

1. Prepare the ingredients. Peel and quarter the onions. Rinse, peel, and trim the carrots and celery. This will result in a cleaner, less-cloudy stock and will help infuse the stock with the flavor of the vegetables. Add herbs and spices.

2. Start with cold water. Add only enough cold water to barely cover the ingredients in the pot. Too much water will dilute the stock's flavor. Be sure the water is cold. Pouring hot water over chicken or meat will release specks of protein that will make the stock cloudy. Don't add salt. The stock will concentrate during cooking, so it doesn't need salt. Instead, add salt to the final soup recipe so that you can control the amount of sodium.

3. Simmer and skim. As soon as the water in the stockpot comes to a boil, reduce the heat to a simmer. Simmering means the liquid is not quite boiling, but there should be noticeable small bubbles that continually rise to the surface. You will also notice gray foam, impurities, rising to the surface of the stock. Gently remove and discard this foam with a spoon, ladle, or skimmer. If you don't remove the foam, it will eventually reincorporate into the stock, making it cloudy and affecting the taste. Continue to allow the stock to simmer for several hours to develop a rich flavor.

4. Strain. Place a fine sieve over a large bowl or pot in the sink. Start by straining the stock in batches, transferring it from the pot to the sieve with a ladle until the stockpot is light enough to lift.

5. Remove the fat. Cool the stock to room temperature, then return the strained stock to the stockpot or divide it among smaller containers and place it in the refrigerator. As the stock chills, the fat will solidify on top, making it easy to remove with a large spoon.

6. Reduce. Once the fat is removed, the stock is ready to use. However, it's a good idea to reduce all of it right away to concentrate the flavors and save on storage space. Bring the stock to a simmer again, and let it reduce by half the volume.

7. Store. Cool up to 4 quarts of stock in a stockpot in the refrigerator. Reduced stock takes on the consistency of gelatin after it has chilled, making it easy to handle. Just keep it in a tub, and spoon it out as needed. Stock will keep in the refrigerator up to a week and in the freezer up to 3 months. Just pour the stock into airtight containers, filling them three-fourths full to allow room for the liquid to expand as it freezes. Freeze smaller amounts in ice-cube trays; then remove the cubes from the trays, and store them in zip-top freezer bags.

No Time to Chill

Chilling the stock overnight makes degreasing a cinch because the fat solidifies on top. But it's also fine to proceed with a recipe right after making the stock. Our Test Kitchens' favorite methods involve either a zip-top plastic bag or a fat separator cup. The cup is made of inexpensive plastic or glass and has a spout at the base. When you pour out the stock, the fat floating on the top stays behind. The zip-top bag works similarly. Pour stock into a bag and seal; and let stand 10 minutes (fat will rise to the top). Carefully snip off 1 bottom corner of the bag. Drain stock into a container, stopping before the fat layer reaches the opening; discard the fat.

How to Make Brown Chicken Stock

Brown stock has deeper flavor than white stock, and the procedure involves caramelizing chicken and vegetables in the oven for half the cooking time, and then putting them in a stockpot to simmer during the second half of cooking.

1. Roasting the vegetables and chicken until browned creates a deep, rich caramelized flavor.

2. The browned bits from the pan add even more flavor. Deglaze the pan by adding water and scraping up the flavorful bits.

3. Simmer the stock ingredients for 1½ hours. Then strain through a fine sieve.

4. Skim the fat from the stock after the stock has chilled for 8 hours or overnight.

Brown Chicken Stock

Use a pan large enough to roast the chicken and all the vegetables in a single layer. If the pan is too small, the chicken won't brown properly.

Yield: 10 cups (serving size: 1 cup)

¼ pound fennel stalks, cut into 2-inch-thick pieces

3 carrots, cut into 2-inch-thick pieces

1 celery stalk, cut into 2-inch-thick pieces

1 medium onion, peeled and quartered

6 pounds chicken pieces

½ teaspoon black peppercorns

6 parsley sprigs

5 thyme sprigs

2 bay leaves

16 cups cold water, divided

1. Preheat oven to 400°.
2. Arrange first 4 ingredients in bottom of a broiler or roasting pan; top with chicken. Bake at 400° for 1½ hours; turn chicken once every 30 minutes (chicken and vegetables should be very brown).
3. Place peppercorns, parsley, thyme, and bay leaves in an 8-quart stockpot. Remove vegetables and chicken from broiler pan; place in stockpot. Discard drippings from broiler pan, leaving browned bits. Place broiler pan on stovetop; add 4 cups water. Bring to a boil over medium-high heat. Reduce heat; simmer 10 minutes, scraping pan to loosen browned bits.
4. Pour contents of pan into stockpot. Add remaining 12 cups water; bring to a boil over medium-high heat. Reduce heat; simmer, uncovered, 1½ hours, skimming surface occasionally to remove foam.
5. Strain stock through a fine sieve into a large bowl. Reserve chicken for another use; discard remaining solids. Cool stock to room temperature. Cover and chill stock 8 hours. Skim solidified fat from surface of stock; discard fat. Refrigerate stock in an airtight container for up to 1 week, or freeze for up to 3 months.

Calories 31; Fat 1.1g (sat 0.3g, mono 0.4g, poly 0.2g); Protein 4.7g; Carb 0.4g; Fiber 0.1g; Chol 15mg; Iron 0.3mg; Sodium 19mg; Calc 4mg

Vegetable Stock

This all-purpose vegetable stock has woodsy undertones. Improvise with a variety of vegetables, but avoid bitter ones such as eggplant or dark greens, which can compete with the flavors of the finished dish.

Yield: 6 cups (serving size: 1 cup)

12 cups cold water

1 (8-ounce) package mushrooms, sliced

1 cup chopped onion

¾ cup chopped carrot

½ cup coarsely chopped celery

½ cup chopped parsnip

2 bay leaves

2 thyme sprigs

1 whole garlic head, halved

1. Combine all ingredients in a stockpot; bring to a boil. Reduce heat, and simmer, uncovered, until reduced to 6 cups (about 1 hour). Strain stock through a fine sieve into a large bowl; discard solids. Cool stock to room temperature. Refrigerate stock in an airtight container for up to 1 week, or freeze for up to 3 months.

Calories 8; Fat 0.1g (sat 0g, mono 0g, poly 0.1g); Protein 0.3g; Carb 1.7g; Fiber 0.3g; Chol 0mg; Iron 0.1mg; Sodium 2mg; Calc 7mg

Beef Stock

Beef stock (made from beef and veal bones) is the basis of many classic European sauces. It makes quick, light, deeply flavored pan sauces. Find oxtails at a butcher shop.

Yield: 10 cups (serving size: 1 cup)

3½ pounds meaty beef bones (such as oxtail)

3 cups coarsely chopped celery

1½ cups chopped carrot (about ¾ pound)

2 tablespoons tomato paste

3 medium onions, peeled and halved (about 1½ pounds)

20 cups cold water

1. Preheat oven to 400°.

2. Arrange bones in an even layer in a shallow roasting pan. Bake at 400° for 45 minutes or until browned.

3. Transfer bones to an 8-quart stockpot. Add celery, carrot, tomato paste, and onions to pot; stir well to combine. Pour cold water over mixture; bring mixture to a simmer. Reduce heat, and simmer, uncovered, 5 hours, skimming surface occasionally to remove foam.

4. Strain stock through a fine sieve into a large bowl; discard solids. Cool stock to room temperature. Cover and chill stock 8 to 24 hours. Skim solidified fat from surface; discard. Refrigerate stock in an airtight container for up to 1 week, or freeze for up to 3 months.

Calories 8; Fat 0.3g (sat 0.1g, mono 0.1g, poly 0g); Protein 0.7g; Carb 0.7g; Fiber 0.1g; Chol 2mg; Iron 0.1mg; Sodium 9mg; Calc 4mg

Arrange the bones in an even layer in a shallow roasting pan. Bake at 400° for 45 minutes or until browned.

Reduce heat, and simmer, uncovered, 5 hours, skimming the surface occasionally to remove the foam.

Shellfish Stock

Next time you cook lobster, save the shells to prepare this stock. You can also make the stock with an equivalent quantity of crab shells, or use a combination of crab and lobster shells. For a less expensive option, use shrimp shells. Straining the stock twice makes for a smooth, clean-tasting final product.

Yield: 10 cups (serving size: 1 cup)

2½ pounds lobster shells (about 4 small lobsters)

2 cups coarsely chopped celery

2 cups coarsely chopped fennel bulb

1 cup coarsely chopped carrot

2 tablespoons no-salt-added tomato paste

2 medium onions, peeled and halved (about 1 pound)

5 quarts water

1. Preheat oven to 450°.
2. Arrange shells in an even layer in a shallow roasting pan. Bake at 450° for 30 minutes or until toasted.
3. Transfer shells to an 8-quart stockpot. Add celery, fennel, carrot, tomato paste, and onions to pot; stir well to combine. Pour water over vegetable mixture; bring to a boil. Reduce heat, and simmer, uncovered, 4 hours, skimming surface occasionally to remove foam.
4. Strain stock through a sieve into a large bowl; discard solids. Strain again through a paper towel-lined sieve. Cool stock to room temperature. Cover and chill stock. Refrigerate stock in an airtight container for up to 2 days, or freeze for up to 3 months.

Calories 9; Fat 0.1g (sat 0.0g, mono 0.0g, poly 0.0g); Protein 1.3g; Carb 0.8g; Fiber 0.2g; Chol 4mg; Iron 0.1mg; Sodium 35mg; Calc 15mg

Corn Stock

This is a great way to use leftover corn cobs (cut the kernels off first, and use them in a soup or salad). Corn stock adds a fresh, sweet taste to corn or seafood chowders, tortilla soup or other Mexican-flavored soups, and vegetable soups. This version takes a shortcut by using canned vegetable broth as a base.

Yield: 10 cups (serving size: 1 cup)

Cooking spray

1 small unpeeled onion, sliced

2 garlic cloves, minced

3 scraped corn cobs

8 (14½-ounce) cans vegetable broth

1. Coat a large Dutch oven with cooking spray, and place over medium-high heat until hot. Add onion and garlic; sauté 5 minutes.
2. Add corn cobs and broth; bring to a boil. Reduce heat, and simmer, uncovered, 1 hour. Remove from heat; cover and let stand 30 minutes. Strain mixture through a sieve into a large bowl; discard solids. Cool stock to room temperature. Cover and chill stock. Refrigerate stock in an airtight container for up to 2 days, or freeze for up to 3 months.

Calories 22; Fat 0.1g (sat 0g, mono 0g, poly 0g); Protein 0.2g; Carb 5.4g; Fiber 0.2g; Chol 0mg; Iron 0mg; Sodium 316mg; Calc 2.8mg

Essential Techniques for Making Soups

Use these cooking tips and techniques as a quick reference when making soup.

1. Sauté. Sautéing vegetables fills the kitchen with a wonderful aroma. Slowly cook a combination of vegetables (such as onions, garlic, carrots, and celery) plus herbs and spices in a small amount of fat (butter, oil, or even bacon drippings for a salty, smoky flavor) until the vegetables are tender. It's a good idea to pay close attention and to stir constantly with a wooden spoon to keep the food from burning. The goal is to cook the vegetables until they're tender. If the vegetables burn, they may add a bitter, undesirable flavor to the soup. It's much better to start over at this point in the recipe rather than compromising the flavor of the whole pot of soup.

2. Caramelize and brown. Vegetables contain natural sugars. As vegetables slowly cook, these sugars are released and begin to turn the vegetables brown, or caramelize them. This is different from scorching or burning. As the vegetables brown, they begin to release rich flavors. It's the blending of these flavors that's the foundation of soups. Soup and stew recipes that call for beef, pork, or game often direct you to brown the meat before continuing with the recipe. Cook the meat in small batches so that it gets a nice brown color on all sides. This browning process contributes deep flavor to the soup. Don't rush and try to cook all of the meat at one time. If you do, the meat will steam rather than brown, and you won't have the rich flavor or brown color that is so important to the overall taste and appearance of the soup.

3. Deglaze. It's important not to leave any concentrated flavor in the bottom of a skillet or pan. Add a small amount of liquid—stock, broth, water, wine, or a combination—to loosen the browned bits of caramelized food. These browned bits contribute greatly to the flavor of the soup. Besides that, leaving the browned bits on the bottom of the pan may cause the soup or stew to stick, which will cause burning.

4. Simmer. Once you have the flavor base for the soup, it's time to add the remaining ingredients. Begin with those that have to cook the longest, such as beans, rice, potatoes, and the remaining liquid. Cover the pot, and cook over low heat until done. Stir the soup occasionally to make sure that nothing sticks to the bottom of the pan.

5. Thicken. Some soups have a clear, thin broth. Others, such as chowders and cream soups, are thick and creamy. To reduce the fat but maintain the flavor and texture of a cream soup, combine a small amount of cream, evaporated fat-free milk, or reduced-fat milk with flour, and stir this mixture into the soup near the end of cooking time. Remember to bring the soup back to a boil, reduce the heat, and cook, stirring occasionally, at least 10 to 15 minutes or until thick. Otherwise, the soup may taste like flour and be too thin. For bean, lentil, or vegetable soups, remove about 1 cup of the soup near the end of the cooking time. Puree it in a blender or mash it with a fork or potato masher, and stir it back into the soup.

Deglaze

Simmer

Thicken

Freezing Soups & Stews

1. Chill. To keep food safe, cool freshly cooked dishes quickly before freezing. Putting foods that are still warm in the freezer can raise the temperature, causing surrounding frozen items to partially thaw and refreeze, which can alter the taste and texture of some foods. Place food in a shallow, wide container and refrigerate, uncovered, until cool. To chill soup or stew even faster, pour it into a metal bowl and set in an ice bath—a larger bowl filled halfway with ice water. Stir occasionally. For stews, braises, or other semi-liquid dishes with some fat content, chill completely, and then skim the fat from the top before freezing. Fat spoils over time in the freezer and shortens a dish's frozen shelf life.

2. Store. Avoid freezer burn by using moisture-proof zip-top plastic bags and wrap. Remove the air from bags before sealing. Store soups and stews in freezer bags, which can be placed flat and freeze quickly. Store foods in small servings, no more than 1 quart, to help them freeze quickly. This also allows you to defrost only what you need. Use a permanent marker to label each container with the name of the dish, volume or weight if you've measured it, and the date you put it in the freezer.

3. Freeze quickly. The quicker food freezes, the better its quality once thawed. Do not crowd the freezer—arrange containers in a single layer in the freezer to allow enough room for air to circulate around them so food will freeze rapidly. Food frozen slowly forms large ice crystals that may turn the food mushy. Most cooked dishes will keep for two to three months in the freezer. Use a freezer thermometer to ensure that your unit remains at 0° or below.

4. Defrost. You can defrost food in the microwave but allowing enough time for it to defrost in the refrigerator (roughly 5 hours per pound) is better. To avoid the risk of contamination, never defrost food at room temperature.

10 Ways to Dress Up Soup with Style

1. For casual meals, serve soup right from the pot. For formal entertaining, use soup tureens.

2. Use your imagination when choosing individual serving bowls. Deep bowls and mugs are good for chunky soups. Wide-rimmed, shallow bowls are ideal for smooth, creamy soups or for clear broth soups where the broth itself creates its own beauty.

3. Consider nontraditional serving dishes such as a cup and saucer for a first-course soup.

4. To keep the soup from cooling too quickly, rinse the serving bowls with hot water just before ladling. For chilled soups, place the empty bowls in the refrigerator about 30 minutes before filling.

5. Use simple garnishes, such as lemon or lime wedges or grated, shredded, or shaved cheeses. Sometimes the ingredients used in the recipe can be used to garnish the soup as well as enhancing flavor and texture.

6. If the soup calls for fresh herbs, set aside a few extra sprigs before beginning. Use the sprigs later as a garnish, or chop a little extra to scatter over the soup before serving.

7. For creamy or pureed soups, garnish with whole, thinly sliced, or chopped vegetables.

8. A dollop of reduced-fat sour cream or yogurt can tame the heat and add the finishing touch to a bowl of spicy soup. Or it can be swirled into a creamy soup for a decorative presentation.

9. Sprinkle soup with homemade or store-bought croutons or fresh tortillas cut into strips. Or simply lay a breadstick across the rim of the soup bowl.

10. Mound rice or pasta in the center of a bowl (or even off-center), and ladle the soup around it, taking care not to completely cover the rice or pasta.

quick
& easy

Tomato-Basil Soup

Fresh tomato and basil are the stars of this classic summertime tomato soup recipe. Low-fat milk and light cream cheese keep it healthy.

Yield: 8 servings (serving size: 1 cup soup and 1 bread slice)

4 cups chopped seeded peeled tomato (about 4 large)

4 cups low-sodium tomato juice

⅓ cup fresh basil leaves

1 cup 1% low-fat milk

¼ teaspoon salt

¼ teaspoon cracked black pepper

½ cup (4 ounces) ⅓-less-fat cream cheese, softened

Basil leaves, thinly sliced (optional)

8 (½-inch-thick) slices diagonally cut French bread baguette

1. Bring tomato and juice to a boil in a large saucepan. Reduce heat; simmer, uncovered, 30 minutes.

2. Place tomato mixture and basil in a blender or food processor; process until smooth. Return pureed mixture to pan; stir in milk, salt, and pepper. Add cream cheese, stirring well with a whisk, and cook over medium heat until thick (about 5 minutes). Ladle soup into individual bowls; garnish with sliced basil, if desired. Serve with bread.

NOTE: Refrigerate remaining soup in an airtight container for up to 1 week.

Calories 133; Fat 4.4g (sat 2.4g, mono 1.3g, poly 0.4g); Protein 5.4g; Carb 18.7g; Fiber 1.9g; Chol 12mg; Iron 1.5mg; Sodium 310mg; Calc 77mg

Sun-Dried Tomato Tortellini Soup

The dry-packed tomatoes rehydrate in this quickly made soup, eliminating the need to steep them.

Yield: 6 servings (serving size: about 1½ cups soup)

1½ teaspoons olive oil

1 cup chopped onion

1 cup (¼-inch-thick) sliced carrot

⅔ cup chopped celery

2 garlic cloves, minced

5 cups fat-free, lower-sodium chicken broth

2 cups water

1¼ cups sun-dried tomato halves, packed without oil, chopped (about 3 ounces)

½ teaspoon dried basil

¼ teaspoon freshly ground black pepper

1 bay leaf

3 cups fresh cheese tortellini (about 12 ounces)

1 cup chopped bok choy

1. Heat oil in a large Dutch oven over medium-high heat. Add onion, carrot, celery, and garlic; sauté 5 minutes. Add broth and next 5 ingredients (through bay leaf); bring to a boil. Reduce heat; simmer 2 minutes. Add pasta and bok choy; simmer 7 minutes or until pasta is done. Discard bay leaf.

Calories 262; Fat 5.4g (sat 2.2g, mono 2.0g, poly 0.4g); Protein 13g; Carb 41.2g; Fiber 4.6g; Chol 24mg; Iron 2.2mg; Sodium 719mg; Calc 119mg

MAKE AHEAD TIP

The soup, without the tortellini and bok choy, can be prepared ahead and refrigerated up to seven days, or frozen up to a month. Add the pasta and the bok choy when you reheat the soup for the best results.

Creamy Sweet Potato Soup

Just a bit of Dijon mustard and nutmeg pair beautifully to enhance the rich flavor of sweet potatoes.

Yield: 4 servings (serving size: ¾ cup soup)

2 cups (¼-inch) cubed peeled sweet potato

1½ cups thinly sliced leek (about 1 medium)

1¼ cups fat-free, lower-sodium chicken broth, divided

⅔ cup evaporated fat-free milk

1½ teaspoons Dijon mustard

Dash of white pepper

Dash of ground nutmeg

Chopped leek (optional)

1. Combine sweet potato, sliced leek, and ¼ cup broth in a 1½-quart casserole; stir well. Cover, and microwave at HIGH 10 minutes, stirring after 5 minutes. Place sweet potato mixture in a blender or food processor; process until smooth. Add 1 cup broth, evaporated milk, and remaining ingredients except chopped leek; process 30 seconds or until blended. Garnish with chopped leek, if desired. Serve warm.

Calories 118; Fat 0.2g (sat 0.1g, mono 0g, poly 0.1g); Protein 6g; Carb 23.7g; Fiber 2.6g; Chol 2mg; Iron 1.2mg; Sodium 315mg; Calc 163mg

FLAVOR TIP

Use freshly grated nutmeg to get the most of its warm, slightly sweet flavor and great aroma. Buy whole nutmeg, and use a Microplane® or another fine spice grater. A little goes a long way!

Creamy Pumpkin Soup

Top with Crisp Croutons (page 258), if desired.

Yield: 5 servings (serving size: 1 cup soup)

2 teaspoons butter

1 cup chopped onion

¾ teaspoon dried rubbed sage

½ teaspoon curry powder

¼ teaspoon ground nutmeg

3 tablespoons all-purpose flour

3 (10½-ounce) cans fat-free, lower-sodium chicken broth

1 tablespoon tomato paste

¼ teaspoon salt

3 cups cubed peeled fresh pumpkin (1 pound)

1 cup chopped peeled McIntosh or other sweet cooking apple

½ cup evaporated fat-free milk

Sage sprigs (optional)

1. Melt butter in a Dutch oven over medium heat. Add onion; sauté 3 minutes. Add sage, curry powder, and nutmeg; cook 30 seconds. Stir in flour; cook 30 seconds. Add broth, tomato paste, and salt, stirring well with a whisk. Stir in pumpkin and apple; bring to a boil. Cover, reduce heat, and simmer 25 minutes or until pumpkin and apple are tender, stirring occasionally. Remove from heat; cool slightly.

2. Place mixture in a blender or food processor; process until smooth. Return mixture to Dutch oven; add milk. Cook until thoroughly heated. Garnish with sage sprigs, if desired.

Calories 133; Fat 3g (sat 1.4g, mono 0.9g, poly 0.3g); Protein 7.5g; Carb 21.8g; Fiber 1.7g; Chol 5mg; Iron 1.7mg; Sodium 240mg; Calc 114mg

INGREDIENT TIP

If you can't find McIntosh apples, try sweet cooking apples like Macoun or Empire apples.

Hot and Sour Soup with Shrimp

Fresh lemon juice lends a tangy, sour flavor to this soup. Add more juice, if you like.

Yield: 4 servings (serving size: 1¾ cups soup)

3 cups fat-free, lower-sodium chicken broth

½ cup presliced mushrooms

2 teaspoons lower-sodium soy sauce

1 (8-ounce) can sliced bamboo shoots, drained

2½ tablespoons fresh lemon juice

1 teaspoon white pepper

1½ pounds medium shrimp, peeled and deveined

1½ cups reduced-fat firm tofu (about 8 ounces), drained and cut into 1-inch cubes

1 tablespoon cornstarch

2 tablespoons water

1 large egg white, beaten

¼ teaspoon chili oil

2 tablespoons chopped green onions

1. Combine first 4 ingredients in a large saucepan; bring to a boil. Reduce heat, and simmer 5 minutes. Add juice, pepper, shrimp, and tofu to pan; bring to a boil. Cook 2 minutes or until shrimp are almost done. Combine cornstarch and water in a small bowl, stirring until smooth. Add cornstarch mixture to pan; cook 1 minute, stirring constantly with a whisk. Slowly drizzle egg white into pan, stirring constantly. Remove from heat; stir in chili oil and onions.

Calories 241; Fat 5.5g (sat 0.6g, mono 0.5g, poly 1.2g); Protein 37.4g; Carb 9.4g; Fiber 2.8g; Chol 204mg; Iron 4.8mg; Sodium 600mg; Calc 114mg

Spicy Coconut Shrimp Soup

Southeast Asian cuisine is known for balanced tastes. Adding the green onions, basil, and lime juice just before serving brightens the overall taste of the soup. For a spicier finish, stir in an additional ¼ teaspoon red curry paste. Garnish with sliced green onions, if desired.

Yield: 4 servings (serving size: about 1½ cups soup)

3½ cups fat-free, lower-sodium chicken broth

1 cup sliced mushrooms

¼ cup finely chopped red bell pepper

1½ teaspoons light brown sugar

1½ teaspoons fish sauce

½ teaspoon grated peeled fresh ginger

¼ teaspoon red curry paste

1 cup light coconut milk

1 pound large shrimp, peeled and deveined

¼ cup thinly sliced green onions

2 tablespoons thinly sliced fresh basil

2 tablespoons fresh lime juice

1. Combine first 7 ingredients in a large saucepan over medium-high heat; bring to a boil. Cover, reduce heat, and simmer 10 minutes. Stir in coconut milk; cook 2 minutes or until hot. Add shrimp to pan; cook 3 minutes or until shrimp reach desired degree of doneness. Remove pan from heat; stir in onions, basil, and juice.

Calories 193; Fat 5.3g (sat 3.3g, mono 0.4g, poly 0.8g); Protein 26.8g; Carb 9.8g; Fiber 1.4g; Chol 172mg; Iron 3.7mg; Sodium 704mg; Calc 85mg

INGREDIENT TIP

You can find red curry paste in the ethnic or gourmet sections of most large supermarkets. This paste is a blend of dried red chile, garlic, and other spices like lemongrass and galangal (Thai ginger). It comes in mild and hot versions, so adjust the heat to suit your preference.

Chicken, Sausage, and Rice Soup

Make a meal of this comforting soup by adding crackers or warm bread.

Yield: 4 servings (serving size: 1½ cups soup)

Cooking spray

4 ounces hot turkey Italian sausage

2 (2½-ounce) skinless, boneless chicken thighs, cut into ½-inch pieces

1½ cups frozen chopped onion

2 thyme sprigs

⅓ cup chopped celery

⅓ cup chopped carrot

2 (14½-ounce) cans fat-free, lower-sodium chicken broth

1 (3½-ounce) bag boil-in-bag brown rice

1 tablespoon chopped fresh parsley

⅛ teaspoon salt

⅛ teaspoon black pepper

1. Remove casings from sausage. Heat a large saucepan over high heat. Coat pan with cooking spray. Add sausage and chicken to pan; cook 2 minutes, stirring to crumble sausage. Add onion and thyme; cook 2 minutes, stirring occasionally. Add celery, carrot, and broth; bring to a boil.

2. Remove rice from bag; stir into broth mixture. Cover, reduce heat to medium, and cook 7 minutes or until rice is tender. Discard thyme sprigs. Stir in parsley, salt, and pepper.

Calories 219; Fat 5.2g (sat 1.3g, mono 1.6g, poly 1.2g); Protein 17.2g; Carb 26.5g; Fiber 3.9g; Chol 53mg; Iron 1.6mg; Sodium 623mg; Calc 38mg

NUTRITION TIP

Chicken thighs and other dark meat pieces have more iron than white meat. They stay tender better than chicken breasts, and they have more flavor, too.

Pasta e Fagioli

This classic Italian pasta and bean soup is often meatless; our version includes turkey Italian sausage. (Pictured on page 18.)

Yield: 6 servings (serving size: 1 cup soup)

1 tablespoon olive oil

6 ounces hot turkey Italian sausage

1½ tablespoons bottled minced garlic

1 cup water

1 (16-ounce) can fat-free, lower-sodium chicken broth

1 (8-ounce) can no-salt-added tomato sauce

1 cup uncooked small seashell pasta (about 4 ounces)

½ cup grated Romano cheese, divided

1½ teaspoons dried oregano

⅛ teaspoon salt

¼ teaspoon white pepper

2 (15-ounce) cans no-salt-added cannellini or other white beans, drained

Minced fresh parsley (optional)

Crushed red pepper (optional)

1. Heat oil in a large saucepan over medium-high heat. Add sausage and garlic; sauté 2 minutes or until browned, stirring to crumble. Add water, broth, and tomato sauce; bring to a boil. Stir in pasta, ¼ cup cheese, oregano, salt, pepper, and beans; bring to a boil. Cover, reduce heat, and simmer 8 minutes or until pasta is done. Let stand 5 minutes; sprinkle with remaining ¼ cup cheese. Garnish each serving with parsley and red pepper, if desired.

Calories 254; Fat 9.2g (sat 2.2g, mono 1.7g, poly 0.4g); Protein 15g; Carb 27.1g; Fiber 6g; Chol 23mg; Iron 3.4mg; Sodium 570mg; Calc 173mg

Quick Chicken Noodle Soup

Heat the broth mixture in the microwave to jump-start the cooking. Meanwhile, sauté the aromatic ingredients in your soup pot to get this dish under way.

Yield: 6 servings (serving size: about 1 cup soup)

2 cups water

1 (32-ounce) carton fat-free, lower-sodium chicken broth

1 tablespoon olive oil

½ cup prechopped onion

½ cup prechopped celery

½ teaspoon salt

½ teaspoon freshly ground black pepper

1 medium carrot, chopped

6 ounces fusilli pasta

2½ cups shredded skinless, boneless rotisserie chicken breast

2 tablespoons chopped fresh flat-leaf parsley

1. Combine 2 cups water and chicken broth in a microwave-safe dish, and microwave at HIGH 5 minutes.
2. While broth mixture heats, heat a large saucepan over medium-high heat. Add oil to pan; swirl to coat. Add onion, celery, salt, pepper, and carrot; sauté 3 minutes or until almost tender, stirring frequently. Add hot broth mixture and pasta; bring to a boil. Reduce heat; simmer 7 minutes or until pasta is almost al dente. Stir in chicken; cook 1 minute or until thoroughly heated. Stir in parsley.

Calories 237; Fat 4.8g (sat 1g, mono 2.4g, poly 0.9g); Protein 22.9g; Carb 23.9g; Fiber 1.7g; Chol 50mg; Iron 1.8mg; Sodium 589mg; Calc 28mg

INGREDIENT TIP

Though we like the shape of fusilli for this soup, you can also make it with other pasta, such as wide egg noodles or even rice-shaped orzo.

Quick Avgolemono, Orzo, and Chicken Soup

Avgolemono (ahv-goh-LEH-moh-noh) is a tangy Greek soup that combines chicken broth, eggs, and lemon juice. Traditional versions include rice; our interpretation uses orzo. Serve with pita chips.

Yield: 4 servings (serving size: 2 cups soup)

5 cups fat-free, lower-sodium chicken broth

1 cup water

1 teaspoon finely chopped fresh dill

½ cup uncooked orzo (rice-shaped pasta)

4 large eggs

⅓ cup fresh lemon juice

1 cup shredded carrot

¼ teaspoon black pepper

8 ounces skinless, boneless chicken breast, cut into bite-sized pieces

1. Bring broth, 1 cup water, and dill to a boil in a large saucepan. Add orzo. Reduce heat, and simmer 5 minutes or until orzo is slightly tender. Remove from heat.

2. Place eggs and juice in a blender; process until smooth. Remove 1 cup broth from pan with a ladle, making sure to leave out orzo. With blender on, slowly add broth; process until smooth.

3. Add carrot, pepper, and chicken to pan. Bring to a simmer over medium-low heat, and cook 5 minutes or until chicken and orzo are done. Reduce heat to low. Slowly stir in egg mixture; cook 30 seconds, stirring constantly (do not boil).

Calories 222; Fat 6.2g (sat 1.9g, mono 2.2g, poly 0.9g); Protein 24.7g; Carb 16.3g; Fiber 2.5g; Chol 244mg; Iron 2.5mg; Sodium 611mg; Calc 65mg

Broccoli and Chicken Noodle Soup

Count on having dinner on the table in about 40 minutes, and serve this soup the moment it's done for the best results.

Yield: 10 servings (serving size: 1 cup soup)

Cooking spray

2 cups chopped onion

1 cup presliced mushrooms

1 garlic clove, minced

3 tablespoons canola oil

1.1 ounces all-purpose flour (about ¼ cup)

4 cups 1% low-fat milk

1 (14-ounce) can fat-free, lower-sodium chicken broth

4 ounces uncooked vermicelli, broken into 2-inch pieces

2 cups (8 ounces) shredded light processed cheese

4 cups (1-inch) cubed cooked chicken breast

3 cups small broccoli florets (8 ounces)

1 cup half-and-half

1 teaspoon freshly ground black pepper

½ teaspoon salt

1. Heat a Dutch oven over medium-high heat. Coat pan with cooking spray. Add onion, mushrooms, and garlic to pan; sauté 5 minutes or until liquid evaporates, stirring occasionally. Reduce heat to medium; add canola oil to mushroom mixture. Sprinkle mushroom mixture with flour; cook 2 minutes, stirring occasionally. Gradually add milk and broth, stirring constantly with a whisk; bring to a boil. Reduce heat to medium-low; cook 10 minutes or until slightly thick, stirring constantly. Add pasta to pan; cook 10 minutes. Add cheese to pan, and stir until cheese melts. Add chicken and remaining ingredients to pan; cook 5 minutes or until broccoli is tender and soup is thoroughly heated.

Calories 331; Fat 14.5g (sat 5.4g, mono 4.4g, poly 2.1g); Protein 26g; Carb 24.2g; Fiber 1.9g; Chol 65mg; Iron 1.7mg; Sodium 702mg; Calc 303mg

QUICK TIP

If the broccoli florets are large, break into smaller pieces at the stalk instead of chopping them; they'll cook more quickly.

North Woods Bean Soup

Adding turkey kielbasa lends this hearty soup recipe a rich, slow-simmered flavor even though it takes less than 30 minutes to make.

Yield: 5 servings (serving size: about 1½ cups soup)

Cooking spray

1 cup baby carrots, halved lengthwise

1 cup chopped onion

2 garlic cloves, minced

5 ounces turkey kielbasa, halved lengthwise and cut into ½-inch pieces

4 cups fat-free, lower-sodium chicken broth

½ teaspoon dried Italian seasoning

½ teaspoon black pepper

2 (15.8-ounce) cans organic Great Northern beans, drained and rinsed

1 (6-ounce) bag fresh baby spinach leaves

1. Heat a large saucepan over medium-high heat. Coat pan with cooking spray. Add carrots, onion, garlic, and kielbasa; sauté 3 minutes, stirring occasionally. Reduce heat to medium; cook 5 minutes. Add broth, Italian seasoning, pepper, and beans. Bring to a boil, reduce heat, and simmer 5 minutes.

2. Place 2 cups soup in a food processor or blender, and process until smooth. Return pureed mixture to pan. Simmer an additional 5 minutes. Remove soup from heat. Add spinach, stirring until spinach wilts.

Calories 180; Fat 3.6g (sat 0.8g, mono 0.7g, poly 0.5g); Protein 10.4g; Carb 27g; Fiber 9.5g; Chol 18mg; Iron 2.6mg; Sodium 709mg; Calc 108mg

NUTRITION TIP

Organic canned beans are typically lower in sodium than standard canned beans. You can also look for "no-salt-added" canned beans to reduce the sodium even further.

Turkey Soup Provençal

The secret ingredient in this aromatic soup is herbes de Provence. Complete the meal with slices of French bread.

Yield: 4 servings (serving size: 1¼ cups soup)

1 pound ground turkey breast

½ teaspoon dried herbes de Provence, crushed

1 (15-ounce) can no-salt-added cannellini or other white beans, drained and rinsed

1 (14.5-ounce) can fat-free, lower-sodium chicken broth

1 (14.5-ounce) can diced tomatoes with garlic and onion, undrained

4 cups chopped fresh spinach

1. Cook turkey in a large saucepan over medium-high heat until browned, stirring to crumble.

2. Add herbes de Provence, beans, broth, and tomatoes to pan; bring to a boil. Reduce heat, and simmer 5 minutes. Stir in spinach; simmer 5 minutes or until spinach wilts.

Calories 271; Fat 10.2g (sat 2.6g, mono 3.6g, poly 2.3g); Protein 26.6g; Carb 17.4g; Fiber 4.7g; Chol 90mg; Iron 4.7mg; Sodium 641mg; Calc 92mg

INGREDIENT TIP

Herbes de Provence is an assortment of dried herbs that usually includes thyme, sage, rosemary, basil, and savory.

Chipotle Turkey and Corn Soup

Stacking the turkey cutlets, and then thinly slicing them will save you some time during preparation. Chipotle chiles come canned in adobo sauce; use that for the adobo sauce called for in this recipe.

Yield: 4 servings (serving size: 1½ cups soup, 2 tablespoons chips)

1 tablespoon canola oil

1 pound turkey cutlets, cut into thin strips

2 teaspoons adobo sauce

1 to 2 teaspoons chopped canned chipotle chiles in adobo sauce

2 (14-ounce) cans fat-free, lower-sodium chicken broth

1 (14¾-ounce) can cream-style corn

¼ cup chopped fresh cilantro, divided

½ cup crushed tortilla chips (about 1½ ounces)

4 lime wedges

1. Heat oil in a large saucepan over medium-high heat. Add turkey; cook 3 minutes or until browned, stirring occasionally. Stir in adobo sauce, chiles, broth, and corn; bring to a boil. Reduce heat to medium-low; simmer 5 minutes. Stir in 3 tablespoons cilantro. Divide soup evenly among 4 bowls; sprinkle evenly with remaining cilantro and crushed chips. Serve with lime wedges.

Calories 303; Fat 7.6g (sat 0.6g, mono 2.9g, poly 2.3g); Protein 32.2g; Carb 27.4g; Fiber 2.8g; Chol 45mg; Iron 2.4mg; Sodium 561mg; Calcium 23mg

INGREDIENT TIP

You can freeze leftover canned chipotle chiles in the adobo sauce. Package the chiles individually with a little sauce in small plastic freezer bags. Use them in salsas, with pork, or for Mexican-inspired scrambled eggs.

Tequila Pork Chile Verde

An upscale Mexican meal, this surprisingly easy stew combines crispy cornmeal-and-ancho chile-crusted pork tenderloin, tart tomatillos, green chiles, jalapeños, and broth. As it simmers, the flavors mellow until it's time for the final touch: a splash of tequila. Serve with black beans.

Yield: 4 servings (serving size: 1¼ cups soup)

2 teaspoons canola oil

3 tablespoons yellow cornmeal

1 tablespoon ancho chile powder

1 pound pork tenderloin, trimmed and cut into ¾-inch pieces

2 cups coarsely chopped fresh tomatillos (about 12 ounces)

1 (14-ounce) can fat-free, lower-sodium chicken broth

1 (4.5-ounce) can chopped mild green chiles, drained

1 jalapeño pepper, seeded and finely chopped

½ cup thinly sliced green onions

¼ cup chopped fresh cilantro

2 tablespoons tequila

¼ teaspoon salt

1. Heat oil in a large nonstick skillet over medium-high heat.

2. Combine cornmeal and chile powder in a medium bowl. Add pork, tossing to coat. Remove pork from bowl, reserving any remaining cornmeal mixture. Add pork to pan; sauté 5 minutes or until browned. Stir in remaining cornmeal mixture; cook 30 seconds, stirring constantly. Stir in tomatillos, broth, green chiles, and jalapeño; bring to a simmer over medium-low heat. Cook 8 minutes or until tomatillos are tender. Stir in onions and remaining ingredients; simmer 1 minute.

Calories 245; Fat 7.4g (sat 1.7g, mono 3.3g, poly 1.6g); Protein 26.5g; Carb 14.8g; Fiber 3.4g; Chol 74mg; Iron 2.7mg; Sodium 407mg; Calc 30mg

INGREDIENT TIP

Fresh tomatillos have papery husks which peel off easily to reveal what looks like small green tomatoes. They have a tart lemony flavor, and are often cooked to mellow their tang. Choose tomatillos with tightly fitting husks; remove the husks and wash them before using them.

Sausage, Kale, and Bean Soup

Cajun sausage fires a simple five-ingredient soup with smoky spice. Serve with crusty bread.

Yield: 4 servings (serving size: 1¾ cups soup)

2 ounces Cajun smoked sausage, chopped

3 cups fat-free, lower-sodium chicken broth

1 (14.5-ounce) can no-salt-added diced tomatoes, undrained

6 cups coarsely chopped kale (about 8 ounces)

1 (16-ounce) can organic navy beans, drained and rinsed

1. Heat a large saucepan over medium-high heat. Add smoked sausage to pan; cook 2 minutes, stirring occasionally. Add broth and diced tomatoes; bring to a boil over high heat. Stir in kale. Reduce heat, and simmer 4 minutes or until kale is tender. Stir in beans, and cook 1 minute or until soup is thoroughly heated.

Calories 171; Fat 4.9g (sat 1.6g, mono 2g, poly 0.7g); Protein 10.2g; Carb 21.9g; Fiber 6.3g; Chol 10mg; Iron 3.4mg; Sodium 436mg; Calc 150mg

the
classics

French Onion Soup

Once you try this classic onion soup recipe, you'll never try another. It culminates in a rich-tasting soup with melt-in-your-mouth onions and bubbly cheese on top of toasted croutons.

Yield: 8 servings (serving size: 1 cup soup and 1 ounce bread)

2 teaspoons olive oil

4 cups thinly vertically sliced Walla Walla or other sweet onion

4 cups thinly vertically sliced red onion

½ teaspoon sugar

½ teaspoon freshly ground black pepper

¼ teaspoon salt

¼ cup dry white wine

8 cups fat-free, lower-sodium beef broth

¼ teaspoon chopped fresh thyme

8 (1-ounce) slices French bread, cut into 1-inch cubes

8 (1-ounce) slices reduced-fat, reduced-sodium Swiss cheese

1. Heat oil in a Dutch oven over medium-high heat. Add onions to pan; sauté 5 minutes or until tender. Stir in sugar, pepper, and ¼ teaspoon salt. Reduce heat to medium; cook 20 minutes, stirring frequently. Increase heat to medium-high, and sauté 5 minutes or until onion is golden brown. Stir in wine, and cook 1 minute. Add broth and thyme; bring to a boil. Cover, reduce heat, and simmer 2 hours.

2. Preheat broiler.

3. Place bread in a single layer on a baking sheet; broil 2 minutes or until toasted, turning after 1 minute.

4. Place 8 ovenproof bowls on a jelly-roll pan. Ladle 1 cup soup into each bowl. Divide bread evenly among bowls; top each serving with 1 cheese slice. Broil 3 minutes or until cheese begins to brown.

Calories 290; Fat 9.6g (sat 4.8g, mono 1.9g, poly 0.7g); Protein 16.8g; Carb 33.4g; Fiber 3.1g; Chol 20mg; Iron 1.6mg; Sodium 359mg; Calc 317mg

INGREDIENT TIP

When cooked to the point that their natural sugars caramelize, onions darken to a deep golden brown color and take on an interesting sweetness. We prefer to use yellow onions

when caramelizing onions because they aren't too sweet or too pungent. But any type of onion—yellow, white, red, or sweet—works just fine.

Garden Minestrone

You'll truly enjoy our version of minestrone—it pairs fresh vegetables with the rich feel and taste of Asiago cheese.

Yield: 8 servings (serving size: 1½ cups soup)

2 teaspoons olive oil

1 cup chopped onion

2 teaspoons chopped fresh oregano

4 garlic cloves, minced

3 cups chopped yellow squash

3 cups chopped zucchini

1 cup chopped carrot

1 cup fresh corn kernels (about 2 ears)

4 cups chopped tomato, divided

3 (14-ounce) cans fat-free, lower-sodium chicken broth, divided

½ cup uncooked ditalini pasta (very short tube-shaped macaroni)

1 (15.5-ounce) can no-salt-added Great Northern beans, rinsed and drained

1 (6-ounce) package fresh baby spinach

¾ teaspoon salt

½ teaspoon freshly ground black pepper

1 cup (4 ounces) grated Asiago cheese

Coarsely ground black pepper (optional)

1. Heat oil in a Dutch oven over medium-high heat. Add onion to pan; sauté 3 minutes or until softened. Add oregano and garlic; sauté 1 minute. Stir in squash, zucchini, carrot, and corn; sauté 5 minutes or until vegetables are tender. Remove from heat.

2. Place 3 cups tomato and 1 can broth in a blender or food processor; process until smooth. Add tomato mixture to pan; return pan to heat. Stir in remaining 1 cup tomato and remaining 2 cans broth; bring mixture to a boil. Reduce heat, and simmer 20 minutes.

3. Add pasta and beans to pan; cook 10 minutes or until pasta is tender, stirring occasionally. Remove from heat. Stir in spinach, salt, and ½ teaspoon pepper. Ladle soup into individual bowls; top with cheese. Garnish with coarsely ground black pepper, if desired.

Calories 201; Fat 6.8g (sat 2.9g, mono 1g, poly 0.4g); Protein 10.3g; Carb 27.3g; Fiber 7.6g; Chol 13mg; Iron 2.4mg; Sodium 664mg; Calc 187mg

Gazpacho with Avocado and Cumin Chips

Traditional gazpacho is a refreshing hot-weather soup from Spain. Enjoy it here with a few twists, including creamy avocado and cumin-dusted corn chips.

Yield: 8 servings (serving size: ¾ cup soup and 4 Cumin Chips)

1½ cups bottled Bloody Mary mix

1½ cups finely diced tomato

1 cup finely diced yellow bell pepper

¾ cup chopped seeded peeled cucumber

¾ cup finely diced red onion

2 tablespoons fresh lime juice

1 teaspoon red wine vinegar

1 teaspoon Worcestershire sauce

½ teaspoon freshly ground black pepper

2 garlic cloves, crushed

1 (5.5-ounce) can lower-sodium vegetable juice

1 (5.5-ounce) can lower-sodium tomato juice

¾ cup diced peeled avocado

¾ cup chopped green onions

Cumin Chips

1. Combine first 12 ingredients in a large nonaluminum bowl. Cover and chill. Serve chilled with avocado, green onions, and Cumin Chips.

Calories 72; Fat 2.2g (sat 0.3g, mono 1.4g, poly 0.3g); Protein 2g; Carb 12.6g; Fiber 3g; Chol 0mg; Iron 1mg; Sodium 319mg; Calc 27mg

Cumin Chips

Yield: 2 dozen (serving size: 4 chips)

4 (6-inch) corn tortillas, each cut into 6 wedges

Cooking spray

½ teaspoon ground cumin

1. Preheat oven to 350°.

2. Place tortilla wedges on a large baking sheet. Lightly coat wedges with cooking spray, and sprinkle with cumin. Bake at 350° for 10 minutes or until chips are lightly browned and crisp.

Calories 22; Fat 0.4g (sat 0g, mono 0g, poly 0.1g); Protein 0.5g; Carb 4.6g; Fiber 0.6g; Chol 0mg; Iron 0mg; Sodium 3mg; Calc 6mg

Roasted Red Pepper Soup

If you want this soup to be a bit spicier, adjust the amount of hot pepper sauce to suit your taste. Serve with crusty bread and a simple green salad for a quick lunch.

Yield: 6 servings (serving size: 1 cup soup)

8 red bell peppers (about 2¾ pounds)

5 black peppercorns

3 thyme sprigs

1 bay leaf

2 teaspoons olive oil

2 cups diced onion (about 1 large)

1 tablespoon minced fresh garlic

3 cups fat-free, lower-sodium chicken broth

1 cup water

3 tablespoons white wine vinegar

¼ teaspoon hot pepper sauce

¼ teaspoon salt

¼ teaspoon freshly ground black pepper

2 tablespoons chopped fresh chives

1. Preheat broiler.

2. Cut bell peppers in half lengthwise; discard seeds and membranes. Place pepper halves, skin sides up, on a foil-lined baking sheet; flatten with hand. Broil 15 minutes or until blackened. Place in a zip-top plastic bag; seal. Let stand 15 minutes. Peel and chop.

3. Place peppercorns, thyme, and bay leaf on a double layer of cheesecloth. Gather edges of cheesecloth together; tie securely.

4. Heat oil in a large Dutch oven over medium heat. Add onion and garlic; cook 15 minutes or until onion is lightly browned, stirring occasionally. Add bell peppers, cheesecloth bag, broth, 1 cup water, vinegar, and hot pepper sauce to pan. Increase heat to medium-high, and bring to a boil. Cover, reduce heat, and simmer 20 minutes. Remove and discard cheesecloth bag; stir in salt and black pepper. Place half of bell pepper mixture in a blender. Remove center piece of blender lid (to allow steam to escape); secure blender lid on blender. Place a clean towel over opening in blender lid (to prevent splatters). Blend until smooth. Pour pureed mixture into a large bowl; repeat procedure with remaining soup. Sprinkle with chives.

Calories 108; Fat 2.2g (sat 0.3g, mono 1.1g, poly 0.3g); Protein 4.2g; Carb 18.2g; Fiber 5.2g; Chol 0mg; Iron 1.1mg; Sodium 400mg; Calc 30mg

INGREDIENT TIP

Choose bell peppers that feel firm and heavy for their size. Store whole, unwashed bell peppers in a plastic bag in your refrigerator crisper. Since red peppers are near or at peak ripeness, they won't last long; use them within three or four days of purchase.

Black Bean Soup

This soup is topped with a dollop of crema Mexicana, a cultured dairy product. Find it in a Hispanic grocery store, or look for it in the refrigerated case in the ethnic section of your grocery store. You can also substitute sour cream or crème fraîche.

Yield: 4 servings (serving size: 1¼ cups soup)

1 cup dried black beans

2½ tablespoons extra-virgin olive oil, divided

¾ cup chopped onion

7 garlic cloves, minced and divided

2½ cups fat-free, lower-sodium chicken broth

2 cups water

¼ cup no-salt-added tomato paste

1 teaspoon dried oregano

¼ teaspoon salt

¾ teaspoon ground cumin

¼ teaspoon ground red pepper

1 (4-ounce) can chopped green chiles

1 cup fresh cilantro leaves

½ jalapeño pepper, seeded

¼ cup crema Mexicana

3 hard-cooked large eggs, peeled and finely chopped

Fresh cilantro leaves (optional)

1. Sort and wash beans, and place in a large Dutch oven. Cover with water; cover and let stand 8 hours. Drain beans.

2. Heat 1½ teaspoons oil in a Dutch oven over medium heat. Add onion; cook 4 minutes, stirring often. Add 5 garlic cloves; cook 1 minute. Increase heat to medium-high. Add beans, broth, and next 7 ingredients (through chiles); bring to a boil. Cover, reduce heat, and simmer 1 hour or until beans are tender. Let stand 10 minutes.

3. Place half of bean mixture in a blender. Remove center piece of blender lid (to allow steam to escape); secure blender lid on blender. Place a clean towel over opening in blender lid (to prevent splatters). Blend until smooth. Pour into a large bowl. Repeat procedure with remaining mixture. Return soup to pan; cook 5 minutes, stirring often.

4. Finely chop 1 cup cilantro and jalapeño. Combine remaining 2 tablespoons oil, remaining 2 garlic cloves, cilantro, jalapeño, and crema. Ladle 1¼ cups soup into each of 4 bowls; top each with 2 tablespoons crema mixture. Sprinkle soup evenly with eggs. Garnish with cilantro leaves, if desired.

Calories 378; Fat 15.4g (sat 2.5g, mono 8.3g, poly 1.4g); Protein 17.6g; Carb 41.3g; Fiber 6.2g; Chol 167mg; Iron 4.3mg; Sodium 644mg; Calc 63mg

Borscht

There are several different versions of this Russian soup. Unlike this interpretation, many are chunky. If you puree the soup as the recipe directs, you don't have to worry about precision when you're chopping. The simplest way to peel celeriac is to remove the rough, knobby skin with a sharp chef's knife.

Yield: 8 servings (serving size: 1½ cups soup)

1 tablespoon canola oil

1½ cups button mushrooms, thinly sliced

1¾ cups chopped onion

1¾ cups chopped peeled celeriac (celery root)

⅓ cup chopped carrot

⅓ cup chopped parsnip

1 tablespoon tomato paste

7 cups water

½ cup light beer

2½ cups shredded red cabbage

2 cups chopped peeled baking potato

2 garlic cloves, crushed

12 ounces sliced peeled beets

3 tablespoons cider vinegar

2 teaspoons sugar

1 teaspoon kosher salt

¼ teaspoon freshly ground black pepper

½ cup sour cream

2 tablespoons chopped fresh dill

1. Heat oil in a large Dutch oven over medium heat. Add mushrooms to pan; cook 5 minutes, stirring frequently. Add onion; cook 6 minutes. Add celeriac, carrot, and parsnip; cook 4 minutes or until onion is tender, stirring occasionally. Stir in tomato paste. Add 7 cups water and beer; stir well. Reduce heat, and simmer 5 minutes. Stir in cabbage, potato, garlic, and beets; bring to a boil. Reduce heat, and simmer 20 minutes or until vegetables are tender, stirring occasionally. Remove from heat.

2. Place half of beet mixture in a blender. Remove center piece of blender lid (to allow steam to escape); secure blender lid on blender. Place a clean towel over opening in blender lid (to avoid splatters). Blend until smooth. Pour into a large bowl. Repeat procedure with remaining beet mixture. Stir in vinegar, sugar, salt, and pepper. Ladle 1½ cups soup into each of 8 bowls; top each serving with 1 tablespoon sour cream and ¾ teaspoon dill.

Calories 164; Fat 5.1g; (sat 2.1g, mono 2g, poly 0.8g); Protein 3.7g; Carb 26.5g; Fiber 4.2g; Chol 6mg; Iron 1.1mg; Sodium 345mg; Calc 64mg

INGREDIENT TIP

Fresh beets offer great color, flavor, and texture, but preparing them can be intimidating because of their proclivity for staining. To protect your hands, use disposable latex gloves purchased from the drugstore. They're thin enough to allow dexterity while keeping the beets from staining your skin.

Split Pea Soup with Rosemary

For the best flavor, make this soup with the Vegetable Stock on page 13. If you use canned broth instead of the homemade stock, omit the added salt in the recipe.

Yield: 6 servings (serving size: 1 cup soup)

1½ cups green split peas

2 teaspoons olive oil, divided

2 cups chopped onion

1 cup diced carrot

1 bay leaf

1 tablespoon minced garlic cloves, divided (about 3 cloves)

1 tablespoon minced fresh rosemary, divided

1 teaspoon paprika

¼ teaspoon black pepper

1 tablespoon tomato paste

1 tablespoon lower-sodium soy sauce

4 cups water

2 cups Vegetable Stock or 1 (14½-ounce) can organic vegetable broth

1 teaspoon salt

¼ cup chopped fresh parsley

¼ cup reduced-fat sour cream

1. Sort and wash peas; cover with water to 2 inches above peas, and set aside. Heat 1 teaspoon oil in a Dutch oven over medium-high heat. Add onion, carrot, and bay leaf; sauté 5 minutes, stirring frequently. Add 2 teaspoons garlic, 1 teaspoon rosemary, paprika, and pepper; cook 3 minutes. Add tomato paste and soy sauce; cook until liquid evaporates, scraping pan to loosen browned bits.

2. Drain peas. Add peas, 4 cups water, Vegetable Stock, and salt to onion mixture; bring to a boil. Cover, reduce heat to medium-low, and simmer 1 hour, stirring often. Discard bay leaf. Place half of soup in blender or food processor; process until smooth. Pour pureed soup into a large bowl. Repeat procedure with remaining soup.

3. Combine remaining 1 teaspoon oil, remaining 1 teaspoon garlic, remaining 2 teaspoons rosemary, and parsley. Stir parsley mixture into soup. Spoon soup into bowls; top each with sour cream.

Calories 233; Fat 3.5g (sat 1.1g, mono 1.6g, poly 0.5g); Protein 13.7g; Carb 38.7g; Fiber 4.8g; Chol 4mg; Iron 2.9mg; Sodium 559mg; Calc 65mg

Loaded Potato Soup

Based on a casual dining classic, this soup has a terrific balance of flavors—a creamy base with crunchy, salty bacon, the intense flavor of cheddar, and a bit of pungent onion.

Yield: 4 servings (serving size: about 1¼ cups soup)

4 (6-ounce) red potatoes

2 teaspoons olive oil

½ cup prechopped onion

1¼ cups fat-free, lower-sodium chicken broth

3 tablespoons all-purpose flour

2 cups 1% low-fat milk, divided

¼ cup reduced-fat sour cream

½ teaspoon salt

¼ teaspoon freshly ground black pepper

3 bacon slices, halved

⅓ cup shredded cheddar cheese

4 teaspoons thinly sliced green onions

1. Pierce potatoes with a fork. Microwave at HIGH 13 minutes or until tender. Cut in half; cool slightly.

2. While potatoes cook, heat oil in a saucepan over medium-high heat. Add onion; sauté 3 minutes. Add broth. Combine flour and ½ cup milk; add to pan with remaining 1½ cups milk. Bring to a boil; stir often. Cook 1 minute. Remove from heat; stir in sour cream, salt, and pepper.

3. Arrange bacon on a paper towel on a microwave-safe plate. Cover with a paper towel; microwave at HIGH 4 minutes. Crumble bacon.

4. Discard potato skins. Coarsely mash potatoes into soup. Ladle soup into bowls. Top evenly with cheese, green onions, and bacon.

Calories 325; Fat 11.1g (sat 5.2g, mono 4.5g, poly 0.8g); Protein 13.2g; Carb 43.8g; Fiber 3g; Chol 27mg; Iron 1.3mg; Sodium 670mg; Calc 261mg

Vichyssoise

This version of the classic cold potato-leek soup is also delicious served warm.

Yield: 5 servings (serving size: 1 cup soup)

1 teaspoon canola oil

3 cups diced leek (about 3 large)

3 cups diced peeled baking potato (about 1¼ pounds)

1 (16-ounce) can fat-free, lower-sodium chicken broth

⅔ cup half-and-half

¼ teaspoon salt

⅛ teaspoon black pepper

1 tablespoon minced fresh chives

1. Heat oil in a large saucepan over medium-low heat. Add leek; cover and cook 10 minutes or until soft. Stir in potato and broth, and bring to a boil. Cover potato mixture, reduce heat, and simmer 15 minutes or until the potato is tender. Place potato mixture in a blender or food processor, and process until smooth. Place potato mixture in a large bowl, and cool to room temperature. Stir in half-and-half, salt, and pepper. Cover and chill. Sprinkle soup with minced chives.

Calories 195; Fat 5g (sat 2.5g, mono 0.6g, poly 0.4g); Protein 4.9g; Carb 33.8g; Fiber 3.1g; Chol 12mg; Iron 1.7mg; Sodium 291mg; Calc 77mg

INGREDIENT TIP

Leeks often have sand trapped between their layers, so it's important to rinse them well. Cut the root end and the tough green leaves off, then cut the leek in half vertically. Fan the layers out under cold running water to rinse out any dirt and sand.

Canadian Cheese Soup with Pumpernickel Croutons

A cheese soup that is full of flavor, thanks to the contrast of sharp cheddar and pumpernickel.

Yield: 8 servings (serving size: 1 cup soup and ¼ cup croutons)

3 (1-ounce) slices pumpernickel bread, cut into ½-inch cubes

1 onion, peeled and quartered

1 carrot, peeled and quartered

1 celery stalk, quartered

1 teaspoon butter

3.4 ounces all-purpose flour (about ¾ cup)

2 (16-ounce) cans fat-free, lower-sodium chicken broth, divided

3 cups 2% reduced-fat milk

½ teaspoon salt

½ teaspoon paprika

½ teaspoon freshly ground black pepper

1½ cups (6 ounces) shredded reduced-fat sharp cheddar cheese

1. Preheat oven to 375°.

2. Place bread cubes on a jelly-roll pan, and bake at 375° for 15 minutes or until toasted.

3. While croutons bake, place onion, carrot, and celery in a food processor, and pulse until chopped. Melt butter in a large saucepan over medium-high heat. Add vegetables; sauté 5 minutes or until tender.

4. Lightly spoon flour into a dry measuring cup; level with a knife. Gradually add 1 can of broth to flour in a medium bowl; stir well with a whisk. Add flour mixture to pan. Stir in remaining 1 can of broth; bring to a boil. Reduce heat to medium, and cook 10 minutes or until thick. Stir in milk, salt, paprika, and pepper; cook 10 minutes. Remove from heat; add cheese, stirring until cheese melts. Ladle soup into bowls, and top with croutons.

Calories 203; Fat 6.8g (sat 3.8g, mono 1.9g, poly 0.4g); Protein 13.2g; Carb 21.9g; Fiber 1.8g; Chol 23mg; Iron 1.1mg; Sodium 671mg; Calc 318mg

Fiery Tofu and Coconut Curry Soup

Coconut and curry are an unbeatable, enduring combination. In this soup, they play off one another well, enhanced by a little sweetness from brown sugar and the sour tang of lime.

Yield: 6 servings (serving size: 1⅓ cups soup)

2 tablespoons canola oil

2 teaspoons minced garlic

¼ cup red curry paste

1 tablespoon dark brown sugar

2 cups light coconut milk

3¾ cups organic vegetable broth

¼ cup fresh lime juice

¼ cup thinly sliced peeled fresh ginger

2 tablespoons lower-sodium soy sauce

2 cups thinly sliced carrot (about 4)

1½ cups (1-inch) pieces green beans (8 ounces)

2¾ cups (1 [14-ounce] package) water-packed soft tofu, drained and cut into 1-inch cubes

¾ cup fresh cilantro leaves

1. Heat oil in a large saucepan over medium-high heat. Add garlic to pan; sauté 30 seconds or until lightly browned. Add curry paste; sauté 1 minute, stirring constantly. Add brown sugar; cook 1 minute. Stir in coconut milk, broth, juice, ginger, and soy sauce. Reduce heat to low; cover and simmer 1 hour. Add carrot; cook 6 minutes. Add beans, and cook 4 minutes or until vegetables are crisp-tender. Add tofu to pan, and cook 2 minutes. Garnish with cilantro leaves.

Calories 193; Fat 11.5g (sat 4.5g, mono 3.5g, poly 2.8g); Protein 6.7g; Carb 18.6g; Fiber 2.9g; Chol 0.0mg; Iron 1.6mg; Sodium 651mg; Calc 111mg

INGREDIENT TIP

Buy fresh ginger that has smooth skin and feels firm. Use the side of a spoon to peel the ginger easily—it shaves the skin off without wasting too much ginger.

Bouillabaisse

The traditional seafood stew of Provence, a *bouillabaisse* is typically made with tomatoes, onions, wine, olive oil, garlic, herbs, fish and shellfish. Soak up the flavorful broth with a crusty French baguette. While 8 cups of water doesn't seem like much, it's enough to steam the lobsters. If clams are unavailable, substitute an equal amount of mussels.

Yield: 6 servings (serving size: about 3 cups soup)

8 cups water

3 (1¼-pound) whole lobsters

1 tablespoon olive oil

2 cups chopped onion

2 cups coarsely chopped celery

1½ cups coarsely chopped carrot

4 garlic cloves, minced

4 cups coarsely chopped tomato (about 1½ pounds)

½ teaspoon salt

½ teaspoon saffron threads, crushed

½ teaspoon dried thyme

¼ teaspoon black pepper

2 bay leaves

1 pound skinned halibut fillets or other lean white fish fillets, cut into 2-inch pieces

22 small clams, scrubbed (about 1¾ pounds)

30 small mussels, scrubbed and debearded (about 1½ pounds)

½ pound medium shrimp, peeled and deveined

1. Bring water to a boil in an 8-quart stockpot. Plunge lobsters headfirst into water. Return to a boil; cover, reduce heat, and simmer 12 minutes. Remove lobsters from water (do not drain); cool. Remove meat from cooked lobster tails and claws; cut into 1-inch pieces, reserving shells. Cover and refrigerate lobster meat.

2. Return reserved shells to water; bring to a boil. Reduce heat, and simmer 5 minutes. Drain through a colander over a large bowl, reserving broth; discard shells. Wipe pan dry with a paper towel.

3. Heat oil in pan over medium-high heat. Add onion, celery, carrot, and garlic; sauté 5 minutes. Add reserved broth, tomato, salt, saffron, thyme, pepper, and bay leaves; bring to a boil. Reduce heat, and simmer 15 minutes; discard bay leaves. Bring to a boil; add halibut, reduce heat, and simmer 4 minutes. Add clams; cook 1 minute. Add mussels; cook 2 minutes. Add shrimp; cook 3 minutes. Bring to a boil. Add reserved lobster meat, reduce heat, and cook until thoroughly heated. Discard any unopened shells.

Calories 332; Fat 7.1g (sat 1g, mono 2.6g, poly 1.7g); Protein 48.2g; Carb 18.5g; Fiber 4.1g; Chol 146mg; Iron 8.1mg; Sodium 701mg; Calc 162mg

Vatapa

This classic Brazilian dish offers a harmonious balance of tangy, sweet, and spicy flavors. For an authentic touch, sprinkle the soup with chopped peanuts just before serving. Try making this soup with a Brazilian lager or a Mexican beer.

Yield: 6 servings (serving size: about 1⅓ cups soup and ½ cup rice)

Stock:

6 cups water

1 cup chopped onion

¾ cup chopped carrot

1 tablespoon grated peeled fresh ginger

4 garlic cloves, minced

1 pound fish bones

Soup:

Cooking spray

1 cup chopped onion

1 tablespoon brown sugar

1 teaspoon salt

1 tablespoon grated peeled fresh ginger

3 garlic cloves, minced

1 serrano chile, seeded and finely chopped

3 cups chopped seeded peeled tomato

1 (12-ounce) bottle beer

1 (13.5-ounce) can light coconut milk

1 pound grouper or other firm white fish fillets, cut into 1-inch pieces

⅓ cup chopped fresh cilantro

1 tablespoon fresh lime juice

3 cups hot cooked basmati rice

6 lime wedges

1. Combine first 6 ingredients in a large Dutch oven; bring to a boil. Reduce heat, and simmer 30 minutes. Drain stock through a fine sieve into a bowl; discard solids.

2. Wipe pan dry with a paper towel. Heat pan over medium-high heat. Coat pan with cooking spray. Add 1 cup onion, sugar, and salt; sauté 3 minutes. Add 1 tablespoon ginger, 3 garlic cloves, and chile; sauté 30 seconds. Stir in reserved stock, tomato, and beer; bring to a boil. Cook until reduced to 6 cups (about 15 minutes). Stir in coconut milk; bring to a boil. Reduce heat, and simmer 20 minutes, stirring occasionally. Add fish; cook 5 minutes over medium-high heat or until fish flakes easily when tested with a fork or until desired degree of doneness. Stir in cilantro and juice. Serve with rice and lime wedges.

Calories 241; Fat 4.5g (sat 3.5g, mono 0.2g, poly 0.4g); Protein 18.4g; Carb 32.1g; Fiber 1.8g; Chol 28mg; Iron 1.6mg; Sodium 464mg; Calc 50mg

Gramercy Crawfish Gumbo

Traditionally, gumbo starts with a roux–a mixture of flour and fat that cooks slowly until browned. In this recipe, named for a small town in Louisiana, you brown the flour in the oven. This technique provides a deep, nutty flavor without the fat.

Yield: 8 servings (serving size: 1⅓ cups soup and ¾ cup rice)

2.25 ounces all-purpose flour (½ cup)

¼ cup vegetable oil

1 cup finely chopped onion

8 cups water

1½ cups sliced okra pods (about 6 ounces)

¼ cup finely chopped green bell pepper

¼ cup chopped fresh parsley

¼ cup chopped celery leaves

2 to 3 tablespoons Cajun seasoning

1 teaspoon salt

8 garlic cloves, minced

1 (14.5-ounce) can stewed tomatoes, undrained

2 cups cooked crawfish tail meat (about 12 ounces)

1 cup lump crabmeat, shell pieces removed (about ⅓ pound)

1 teaspoon hot sauce

6 cups hot cooked rice

Chopped fresh parsley (optional)

1. Preheat oven to 350°.

2. Weigh or lightly spoon flour into a dry measuring cup; level with a knife. Place flour in a 9-inch pie plate; bake at 350° for 45 minutes or until lightly browned, stirring frequently. Cool on a wire rack.

3. Heat oil in a large Dutch oven over medium-high heat. Add onion; sauté 4 minutes. Stir in browned flour; cook 1 minute, stirring constantly. Gradually stir in water and next 8 ingredients; bring to a boil. Reduce heat; simmer 1 hour.

4. Stir in crawfish, crabmeat, and hot sauce. Bring to a boil; reduce heat, and simmer 25 minutes. Serve gumbo with rice; sprinkle with parsley, if desired.

Calories 325; Fat 8.5g (sat 1g, mono 3.3g, poly 3.4g); Protein 15.5g; Carb 46.7g; Fiber 2.4g; Chol 75mg; Iron 3.5mg; Sodium 597mg; Calc 93mg

SUBSTITUTION TIP

Instead of using bottled Cajun seasoning, you can make your own All that Jazz Seasoning. Combine ¼ cup garlic powder, ¼ cup onion powder, 2 tablespoons paprika, 1 tablespoon ground red pepper, 1 tablespoon black pepper, 1½ teaspoons celery seeds, 1½ teaspoons chili powder, 1 teaspoon salt, 1 teaspoon lemon pepper, and ½ teaspoon ground nutmeg. Yield: 1 cup.

Calories 20; Fat 0.3g (sat 0.1g, mono 0.1g, poly 0.1g); Protein 0.8g; Carb 4.3g; Fiber 1.1g; Chol 0mg; Iron 0.6mg; Sodium 177mg; Calc 18mg

Wonton Soup

To add a little spice, sprinkle with crushed red pepper.

Yield: 6 servings (serving size: 1⅓ cups broth and 6 wontons)

4 cups bagged baby spinach leaves

¾ cup cooked dark-meat chicken (about ½ pound skinless, boneless thighs)

1 tablespoon lower-sodium soy sauce

¾ teaspoon black pepper

¾ teaspoon chopped peeled fresh ginger

¾ teaspoon dark sesame oil

2 garlic cloves, chopped

½ teaspoon salt, divided

40 wonton wrappers

1 large egg white, lightly beaten

2 teaspoons cornstarch

8 cups White Chicken Stock (page 10)

Crushed red pepper (optional)

1. Place first 7 ingredients in a food processor; add ¼ teaspoon salt. Pulse until coarsely chopped.

2. Working with 1 wonton wrapper at a time (cover remaining wrappers with a damp towel to prevent drying), spoon about 1 teaspoon chicken mixture into center of each wrapper. Moisten edges of wrapper with egg white; bring 2 opposite corners to center, pinching points to seal. Bring remaining 2 corners to center, pinching points to seal. Pinch 4 edges together to seal. Place wonton on a baking sheet sprinkled with cornstarch. Repeat procedure with remaining wrappers, chicken mixture, and egg white. Refrigerate on baking sheet 20 minutes.

3. Bring stock to a simmer over medium heat in a large saucepan; add remaining ¼ teaspoon salt. Add wontons; cook 4 minutes or until wontons float to the top, stirring gently. Sprinkle with crushed red pepper, if desired.

Calories 254; Fat 4g (sat 0.9g, mono 1.2g, poly 1.2g); Protein 20.3g; Carb 33g; Fiber 1.7g; Chol 56mg; Iron 3.2mg; Sodium 672mg; Calc 58mg

MAKE AHEAD TIP

To freeze wontons, place them uncooked on a baking sheet. Freeze, and then store in a zip-top plastic bag for up to 2 weeks. Add them, still frozen, to the simmering broth.

Chicken and Rosemary Dumplings

Spoonfuls of seasoned buttermilk biscuit dough form light, fluffy dumplings in this original American dish.

Yield: 6 servings (serving size: 1⅓ cups soup and 2 dumplings)

Soup:

3 cups fat-free, lower-sodium chicken broth

4 cups water

1 pound chicken drumsticks, skinned

1 pound skinless, boneless chicken breast halves

2 thyme sprigs

2 teaspoons olive oil

1½ cups diced carrots

1½ cups chopped celery

1 cup diced onion

2 garlic cloves, minced

¼ teaspoon salt

Dumplings:

5.6 ounces all-purpose flour (about 1¼ cups)

1 tablespoon chopped fresh or ½ teaspoon dried rosemary

2 teaspoons baking powder

¼ teaspoon salt

2 tablespoons butter, softened

½ cup low-fat buttermilk

1 large egg

1.1 ounces all-purpose flour (about ¼ cup)

¼ cup water

Remaining ingredient:

Freshly ground black pepper

1. Combine first 5 ingredients in a large Dutch oven over medium-high heat; bring to a boil. Reduce heat, and simmer, uncovered, 15 minutes or until chicken is done. Remove pan from heat. Remove chicken pieces from broth; cool slightly. Strain broth through a sieve into a large bowl; discard solids. Remove chicken from bones. Discard bones; chop chicken into bite-sized pieces. Set chicken aside.

2. Heat oil in pan over medium-high heat. Add carrots, celery, onion, and garlic; sauté 6 minutes or until onion is tender. Add reserved broth mixture and ¼ teaspoon salt; simmer 10 minutes. Keep warm.

3. Lightly spoon flour into dry measuring cups; level with a knife. Combine 1¼ cups flour, rosemary, baking powder, and ¼ teaspoon salt in a large bowl. Cut in butter with a pastry blender or 2 knives until mixture resembles coarse meal. Combine buttermilk and egg, stirring with a whisk. Add buttermilk mixture to flour mixture, stirring just until combined.

4. Return chopped chicken to broth mixture; bring to a simmer over medium-high heat. Combine ¼ cup flour and ¼ cup water, stirring with a whisk until well blended to form a slurry. Add flour mixture to pan; simmer 3 minutes. Drop dumpling dough, 1 tablespoon per dumpling, into chicken mixture to form 12 dumplings. Cover and cook 7 minutes (do not let broth boil). Sprinkle with black pepper.

Calories 382; Fat 10.5g (sat 4g, mono 3.6g, poly 1.5g); Protein 39.8g; Carb 29.7g; Fiber 2.7g; Chol 148mg; Iron 3.4mg; Sodium 721mg; Calc 167mg

Chipotle Chicken Tortilla Soup

If you like spicy food, you'll love this soup. Serve with Corn Bread Bites (page 257) or purchase corn muffins from your supermarket bakery to round out the meal.

Yield: 4 servings (serving size: 1¼ cups soup and ¼ cup chips)

1 tablespoon canola oil

1½ teaspoons bottled minced garlic

¾ pound chicken breast tenders, cut into bite-sized pieces

1 teaspoon chipotle chile powder

1 teaspoon ground cumin

1 cup water

⅛ teaspoon salt

1 (14-ounce) can fat-free, lower-sodium chicken broth

1 (14.5-ounce) can no-salt-added diced stewed tomatoes, undrained

1 cup crushed baked tortilla chips

¼ cup chopped fresh cilantro

1 lime, cut into 4 wedges

1. Heat oil in a large saucepan over medium-high heat. Add minced garlic and chicken; sauté 2 minutes. Add chile powder and cumin; stir well. Add water, salt, broth, and tomatoes; bring to a boil. Cover, reduce heat, and simmer 5 minutes. Top with tortilla chips and cilantro, and serve with lime wedges.

Calories 227; Fat 5.5g (sat 0.6g, mono 2.5g, poly 1.3g); Protein 23.2g; Carb 20.6g; Fiber 3g; Chol 49mg; Iron 1.8mg; Sodium 440mg; Calc 60mg

Brunswick Stew with Smoked Paprika

This dish is said to have originated in Brunswick County, Virginia, in the 1800s. We spiced it up with a little smoked Spanish paprika (available at gourmet specialty stores and some supermarkets). Use rotisserie chicken to speed up preparation. (Pictured on page 48).

Yield: 6 servings (serving size: about 1½ cups soup)

2 cups (¾-inch) cubed Yukon gold potato

2 cups thinly sliced yellow onion

2 cups frozen corn kernels, thawed

1 cup frozen baby lima beans, thawed

½ cup tomato sauce

2 (14-ounce) cans fat-free, lower-sodium chicken broth

2 bacon slices, cut crosswise into ½-inch strips

3 cups shredded cooked chicken breast

½ teaspoon sweet Spanish smoked paprika

½ teaspoon kosher salt

¼ teaspoon ground red pepper

1. Combine first 7 ingredients in a Dutch oven over medium-high heat; bring to a boil. Reduce heat to low; simmer 30 minutes or until potato is tender, stirring occasionally. Stir in chicken, paprika, salt, and pepper; simmer 15 minutes.

Calories 308; Fat 7.5g (sat 2.4g, mono 3g, poly 1.4g); Protein 29.4g; Carb 31.6g; Fiber 4.9g; Chol 65mg; Iron 2.2mg; Sodium 645mg; Calc 36mg

WINE TIP

Champagne or sparkling wine complement the strong, smoky flavors in the stew. It's a delicious combination that could become a regular autumn weeknight treat.

Creamy Wild-Rice Soup with Smoked Turkey

Wild rice is not really a rice: It is a grass that originated in the Great Lakes area. It still counts as a whole grain, though, and offers more protein than most other whole grains and is richer in antioxidants than white rice.

Yield: 8 servings (serving size: 1 cup soup)

2 teaspoons butter

1 cup chopped carrot

1 cup chopped onion

1 cup chopped green onions

1 teaspoon chopped fresh or ¼ teaspoon dried rosemary

¼ teaspoon black pepper

3 garlic cloves, minced

2 (16-ounce) cans fat-free, lower-sodium chicken broth

1½ cups chopped smoked turkey breast (½ pound)

1 cup uncooked wild rice

1.5 ounces all-purpose flour (about ⅓ cup)

2¾ cups 2% reduced-fat milk

2 tablespoons dry sherry

½ teaspoon salt

1. Melt butter in a Dutch oven over medium-high heat. Add carrot and next 5 ingredients (through garlic). Cook 8 minutes or until browned. Stir in broth, scraping pan to loosen browned bits. Stir in turkey and rice; bring to a boil. Cover, reduce heat, and simmer 1 hour and 15 minutes or until rice is tender.

2. Lightly spoon flour into a dry measuring cup; level with a knife. Combine flour and milk in a small bowl, stirring with a whisk. Add to pan. Cook over medium heat until thick (about 8 minutes), stirring frequently. Stir in sherry and salt.

Calories 206; Fat 4.1g (sat 2.3g, mono 0.8g, poly 0.3g); Protein 13g; Carb 30.2g; Fiber 3.1g; Chol 24mg; Iron 1.2mg; Sodium 629mg; Calc 132mg

Curried Turkey Soup

The sweet flavors of apples and coconut balance the bold spices in this soup. You also get a pleasing crunch from chopped peanuts.

Yield: 11 servings (serving size: 1 cup soup and ¼ cup rice)

Soup:

1 tablespoon butter

4 teaspoons curry powder

1 teaspoon minced peeled fresh ginger

2 garlic cloves, minced

4 (16-ounce) cartons fat-free, lower-sodium chicken broth, divided

2 cups chopped onion

1 cup chopped leek

½ cup diced peeled Golden Delicious apple

½ cup diced carrot

½ cup diced celery

3 cups finely shredded cooked turkey

1 tablespoon lemon juice

⅛ teaspoon white pepper

1 (12-ounce) can evaporated fat-free milk

2.25 ounces all-purpose flour (about ½ cup)

Remaining ingredients:

2¾ cups hot cooked rice

¾ cup diced peeled Golden Delicious apple

⅓ cup chopped dry-roasted peanuts

⅓ cup chopped fresh parsley

⅓ cup flaked sweetened coconut, toasted

1. Melt butter in a large Dutch oven over low heat. Add curry powder, ginger, and garlic; sauté 2 minutes. Add 2 cans of broth, onion, and next 4 ingredients (through celery), and bring to a boil. Reduce heat; simmer 20 minutes or until vegetables are tender.

2. Place half of the vegetable mixture in a food processor, and process until smooth. Spoon into a bowl. Repeat procedure with remaining vegetable mixture. Combine vegetable puree, 1 can of broth, turkey, juice, pepper, and milk in pan, and stir well. Combine remaining 1 can of broth and flour in a bowl. Stir with a whisk; add to vegetable mixture in pan. Bring to a boil; reduce heat, and simmer 10 minutes or until thick, stirring constantly.

3. Spoon ¼ cup rice into each of 11 bowls; top each with 1 cup soup, about 1 tablespoon diced apple, 1½ teaspoons peanuts, 1½ teaspoons parsley, and 1½ teaspoons coconut.

Calories 224; Fat 4.5g (sat 1.9g, mono 1.5g, poly 1g); Protein 16.7g; Carb 29g; Fiber 2.9g; Chol 30mg; Iron 2mg; Sodium 371mg; Calc 134mg

Smoked Ham Soup with White Beans

This high-fiber soup is also great when made with dried cannellini beans. If you have the time, soak the beans overnight instead of using the quick-soak method called for; this will produce creamier beans. Serve with your favorite corn bread recipe, or try the Parmesan-Corn Bread Muffins on page 253.

Yield: 8 servings (serving size: 1¼ cups soup)

1 (16-ounce) package dried navy beans

1 tablespoon olive oil

2 cups chopped yellow onion

4 garlic cloves, minced

8 cups fat-free, lower-sodium chicken broth

4 cups water

2 tablespoons chopped fresh parsley

1 teaspoon chopped fresh thyme

¼ teaspoon salt

¼ teaspoon freshly ground black pepper

2 smoked ham hocks (about 1 pound)

2 bay leaves

1 (14.5-ounce) can petite diced tomatoes, undrained

1. Sort and wash beans; place in a large Dutch oven. Cover with water to 2 inches above beans; bring to a boil. Cook 2 minutes. Remove from heat; cover and let stand 1 hour. Drain.

2. Heat oil in pan over medium heat. Add onion; cook until tender, stirring occasionally. Add garlic, and cook 1 minute, stirring frequently. Add drained beans, broth, and remaining ingredients; bring to a boil. Cover, reduce heat, and simmer 2½ hours or until beans are tender. Discard bay leaves.

3. Remove ham hocks with a slotted spoon, and cool slightly. Remove meat from bones; discard fat, gristle, and bones. Shred meat with 2 forks. Place 1 cup of bean mixture in a blender; process until smooth. Return pureed bean mixture to pan; stir until blended. Stir in meat.

Calories 323; Fat 8.4g (sat 2.6g, mono 4g, poly 1.1g); Protein 22g; Carb 40.7g; Fiber 16.2g; Chol 27mg; Iron 5.6mg; Sodium 558mg; Calc 137mg

Beef-Barley Soup

A generous portion of this hearty soup is satisfying as a one-dish meal. If chuck roast is on sale, purchase a large one and freeze the rest for later. If not, ask your butcher to cut off only the amount you need.

Yield: 4 servings (serving size: 2 cups soup)

Cooking spray

¾ pound boneless chuck roast, trimmed and cut into ½-inch pieces

1½ cups thinly sliced carrot

1½ cups thinly sliced celery

⅔ cup chopped onion

1 (8-ounce) package presliced mushrooms

4 cups fat-free, lower-sodium beef broth

1 bay leaf

⅔ cup uncooked pearl barley

¼ teaspoon salt

½ teaspoon black pepper

1. Heat a Dutch oven over medium-high heat. Coat pan with cooking spray. Add beef to pan; cook 4 minutes or until browned, stirring frequently. Remove beef from pan. Add carrot, celery, onion, and mushrooms to pan; cook 6 minutes or until liquid almost evaporates. Add beef, broth, and bay leaf. Bring to a boil over medium-high heat. Cover, reduce heat, and simmer 1½ hours or until beef is tender, stirring occasionally. Stir in barley; cover and simmer 30 minutes or until barley is tender. Stir in salt and pepper. Discard bay leaf.

Calories 316; Fat 8.7g (sat 2.8g, mono 3.2g, poly 0.7g); Protein 24.2g; Carb 36g; Fiber 8.1g; Chol 52mg; Iron 3.4mg; Sodium 709mg; Calc 55mg

NUTRITION TIP

Barley is best known as an ingredient in beer and soup. Creamy and possessing a fairly neutral flavor when cooked, pearl barley is easy to serve in place of rice. Because it's so starchy, pearl barley can be treated just like Arborio rice for risotto. A great source of fiber, ½ cup of pearl barley offers more than 12 grams.

Beef Goulash

Hungary's national dish is a beef stew flavored with paprika and caraway seeds. Browning the meat first yields the most flavorful result. You can also serve it over egg noodles.

Yield: 8 servings (serving size: 1 cup soup)

1½ pounds boneless chuck roast, trimmed and cut into 1-inch pieces

1.1 ounces all-purpose flour (about ¼ cup)

1¼ teaspoons salt, divided

¾ teaspoon freshly ground black pepper, divided

1 tablespoon butter

4 cups chopped onion (about 2 large)

2 garlic cloves, minced

2 tablespoons paprika

1 tablespoon red wine vinegar

1 cup chopped plum tomato (about 3)

½ teaspoon caraway seeds, crushed

2 bay leaves

½ cup water

1 (14-ounce) can fat-free, lower-sodium beef broth

2½ cups cubed peeled Yukon gold or red potato (about 1 pound)

1 tablespoon fresh lemon juice

1. Dredge beef in flour; sprinkle with ½ teaspoon salt and ¼ teaspoon pepper. Melt butter in a Dutch oven over medium-high heat. Add beef; cook 8 minutes, browning on all sides. Remove beef from pan.

2. Add onion and garlic to pan; sauté 10 minutes or until lightly browned. Stir in paprika and vinegar; cook 2 minutes. Return beef to pan. Add tomato, caraway seeds, and bay leaves; cook 3 minutes. Add ½ teaspoon salt, ¼ teaspoon pepper, ½ cup water, and broth; bring to a boil. Cover, reduce heat, and simmer 1 hour and 45 minutes. Add potato; cover and cook 1 hour and 15 minutes or until very tender. Stir in remaining ¼ teaspoon salt, remaining ¼ teaspoon pepper, and juice. Discard bay leaves.

Calories 242; Fat 6.1g (sat 2.6g, mono 2.3g, poly 0.4g); Protein 24.2g; Carb 22.4g; Fiber 2.5g; Chol 47mg; Iron 2.8mg; Sodium 517mg; Calc 31mg

Beef Daube Provençal

This classic French braised beef, red wine, and vegetable stew is simple and delicious. It offers the homey comfort and convenience of pot roast, yet is versatile and sophisticated enough for entertaining. Garnish with chopped fresh thyme, if desired.

Yield: 6 servings (serving size: about ¾ cup soup and ½ cup noodles)

2 teaspoons olive oil

12 garlic cloves, crushed

1 (2-pound) boneless chuck roast, trimmed and cut into 2-inch cubes

1¼ teaspoons salt, divided

½ teaspoon freshly ground black pepper, divided

1 cup red wine

2 cups chopped carrot

1½ cups chopped onion

½ cup fat-free, lower-sodium beef broth

1 tablespoon no-salt-added tomato paste

1 teaspoon chopped fresh rosemary

1 teaspoon chopped fresh thyme

Dash of ground cloves

1 (14.5-ounce) can no-salt-added diced tomatoes, undrained

1 bay leaf

3 cups hot cooked medium egg noodles (about 4 cups uncooked noodles)

Chopped fresh thyme (optional)

1. Preheat oven to 300°.

2. Heat olive oil in a small oven proof Dutch oven over low heat. Add garlic to pan; cook 5 minutes, stirring occasionally. Remove garlic with a slotted spoon; set aside. Increase heat to medium-high. Add beef to pan. Sprinkle beef with ¼ teaspoon salt and ¼ teaspoon black pepper. Cook 5 minutes, browning on all sides. Remove beef from pan. Add wine to pan, and bring to a boil, scraping pan to loosen browned bits. Add reserved garlic, beef, remaining 1 teaspoon salt, remaining ¼ teaspoon pepper, carrot, and next 8 ingredients (through bay leaf) to pan; bring to a boil. Remove from heat.

3. Cover and bake at 300° for 2½ hours or until beef is tender. Discard bay leaf. Serve over noodles. Garnish with chopped fresh thyme, if desired.

Note: To make in a slow cooker, prepare through Step 2. Place beef mixture in an electric slow cooker. Cover and cook on HIGH for 5 hours.

Calories 539; Fat 26.1g (sat 9.5g, mono 11.3g, poly 1.1g); Protein 38.4g; Carb 30.2g; Fiber 3.1g; Chol 140mg; Iron 4.5mg; Sodium 650mg; Calc 69mg

WINE TIP:

This satisfying beef stew deserves a rich, earthy wine with a soft, thick texture. Try a California syrah.

Hanoi Beef and Rice Noodle Soup (Pho Bo)

Traditionally a northern Vietnamese breakfast specialty, *pho bo* is now eaten throughout the country at any time of day. Charring the meat, ginger, and shallots gives the broth its complexity. Beef oxtail, although bony and tough, is very flavorful, so it's good for making broth. Partially freeze the eye-of-round roast to make it easier to slice. You can also use regular sweet basil in place of Thai basil.

Yield: 6 servings (serving size: ⅓ cup bean sprouts, 1⅓ cups noodles, 2 ounces eye-of-round, and 1⅔ cups broth)

Broth:

3 pounds beef oxtail

¾ cup thinly sliced fresh ginger (about 3 ounces)

⅔ cup coarsely chopped shallots (about 3 medium shallots)

5 quarts water

4 cups coarsely chopped daikon radish (about 1 pound)

2 tablespoons sugar

2 tablespoons Thai fish sauce

1 teaspoon white peppercorns

5 whole cloves

2 star anise

1 large onion, peeled and quartered

1 cinnamon stick

Remaining ingredients:

2 cups vertically sliced onion

12 ounces wide rice stick noodles

2 cups fresh bean sprouts

12 ounces eye-of-round roast, trimmed and cut into ¹⁄₁₆-inch slices

2 cups cilantro leaves

1 cup Thai basil leaves

4 red Thai chiles, seeded and thinly sliced

8 lime wedges

1 tablespoon hoisin sauce (optional)

1. Heat a large stockpot over medium-high heat. Add oxtail, ginger, and shallots; sauté 8 minutes or until ginger and shallots are slightly charred. Add water and next 8 ingredients (through cinnamon stick); bring to a boil. Reduce heat, and simmer 4 hours. Strain broth through a sieve into a large bowl; discard solids. Return broth to pan, and bring to a boil. Reduce heat to medium, and cook until reduced to 10 cups (about 30 minutes). Skim fat from surface; discard fat. Keep very warm.

2. Add sliced onion to broth. Place noodles in a large bowl, and cover with boiling water. Let stand 20 minutes. Drain. Place ⅓ cup bean sprouts in each of 6 soup bowls. Top each serving with 1⅓ cups noodles, and 2 ounces eye-of-round. Return broth to a boil. Carefully ladle 1⅔ cups boiling broth over each serving (boiling broth will cook the meat). Serve with cilantro, basil, chiles, limes, and, if desired, hoisin.

Calories 403; Fat 8.5g (sat 3.3g, mono 3.7g, poly 0.5g); Protein 23.4g; Carb 58g; Fiber 3.5g; Chol 57mg; Iron 3.3mg; Sodium 553mg; Calc 69mg

Harira

During the ninth month of their calendar, Muslims observe the ritual fast of Ramadan. For the entire month, they abstain from eating during the day; in the evening, they take small meals and visit with friends and family. This is a variation of the soup that is traditionally eaten to break the fast at the Ramadan meal.

Yield: 4 servings (serving size: 1¼ cups soup)

1¼ pounds boneless leg of lamb, trimmed and cut into 1-inch cubes

½ teaspoon salt

¼ teaspoon black pepper

1 tablespoon olive oil

1 cup chopped onion

1 tablespoon tomato paste

4 cups water

1 cup drained canned chickpeas (garbanzo beans)

½ teaspoon ground cinnamon

¼ teaspoon ground red pepper

2 cups chopped tomato

½ cup dried small red or brown lentils

½ cup chopped red bell pepper

½ cup hot cooked angel hair pasta (about 1 ounce uncooked pasta)

1 tablespoon minced fresh cilantro

1 tablespoon fresh lemon juice

1. Sprinkle lamb with salt and black pepper. Heat oil in a large Dutch oven over high heat. Add lamb; cook 5 minutes or until browned, stirring occasionally. Add onion; cook 1 minute, stirring frequently. Stir in tomato paste; cook 1 minute, stirring frequently. Stir in water, chickpeas, cinnamon, and ground red pepper. Bring to a boil; reduce heat, and simmer 30 minutes. **2.** Stir in tomato, lentils, and bell pepper. Bring to a boil; reduce heat, and simmer 30 minutes or until lentils are tender. Stir in pasta, cilantro, and juice; cook 1 minute or until thoroughly heated.

Calories 359; Fat 9.2g (sat 2.1g, mono 4.4g, poly 1.5g); Protein 30.4g; Carb 40.6g; Fiber 6.8g; Chol 55mg; Iron 6.3mg; Sodium 544mg; Calc 60mg

hearty stews

Red Bean Stew with Pasta

Elbow macaroni or other short pasta also will work in this Italian-accented dish. Pesto and Parmesan round out the flavor at the end of the cooking time.

Yield: 4 servings (serving size: 1½ cups stew)

1 tablespoon olive oil

1½ cups presliced mushrooms

1 cup diced carrot

1½ cups water

¼ teaspoon black pepper

1 (15-ounce) can kidney beans, rinsed and drained

1 (14.5-ounce) can diced tomatoes, undrained

1 (14-ounce) can fat-free, lower-sodium beef broth

1 cup uncooked ditalini (about 4 ounces short tube-shaped pasta)

2 tablespoons commercial pesto

¼ cup (1 ounce) grated fresh Parmesan cheese

1. Heat olive oil in a Dutch oven over medium-high heat. Add mushrooms and carrot; sauté 4 minutes. Stir in water and next 4 ingredients (through broth). Cover; bring to a boil. Stir in pasta; cook, uncovered, 11 minutes or until pasta is done. Stir in pesto; sprinkle each serving with cheese.

Calories 324; Fat 10.2g (sat 2.3g, mono 4.7g, poly 1.7g); Protein 15.2g; Carb 43.7g; Fiber 10.4g; Chol 6mg; Iron 3.1mg; Sodium 560mg; Calc 150mg

Lentil-Edamame Stew

Fava beans are traditional in this stew, which we updated with edamame. You can also substitute green peas for the edamame. Scoop up the thick stew with Fresh Whole-Wheat Pitas (page 247). Halve the portion if you'd like to serve this as a hearty side dish.

Yield: 4 servings (serving size: about 1 cup stew)

1 cup dried lentils

¾ cup frozen shelled edamame (green soybeans)

2 tablespoons olive oil

1½ cups minced red onion

3 garlic cloves, minced

1 (14.5-ounce) can diced tomatoes, undrained

6 tablespoons fresh lemon juice

1 tablespoon chopped fresh parsley

1 tablespoon chopped fresh mint

½ teaspoon salt

½ teaspoon ground cumin

⅛ teaspoon ground red pepper

⅛ teaspoon ground cinnamon

Dash of ground cloves

Lemon slices (optional)

1. Place lentils in a large saucepan; cover with water to 2 inches above lentils. Bring to a boil; cover, reduce heat, and simmer 20 minutes or until tender. Drain well, and set aside.

2. Place edamame in a small saucepan; cover with water to 2 inches above edamame. Bring to a boil; cook 2 minutes or until edamame are tender. Remove from heat; drain well.

3. Heat oil in a Dutch oven over medium-high heat. Add onion, garlic, and tomatoes to pan; sauté 6 minutes or until onion is translucent, stirring often. Stir in lentils, edamame, juice, and remaining ingredients except lemon slices. Cook 2 minutes or until thoroughly heated, stirring often. Garnish with lemon slices, if desired.

Calories 320; Fat 8g (sat 1.1g, mono 5.2g, poly 1.4g); Protein 18.6g; Carb 48.4g; Fiber 10.7g; Chol 0mg; Iron 5.7mg; Sodium 432mg; Calc 59mg

Wild Mushroom Stew with Gremolata

The Mushroom Stock (page 103) used here also makes a great base for mushroom-barley soup, a savory gravy for mashed potatoes, or a braised bean dish. (Pictured on page 96.)

Yield: 4 servings (serving size: 2 cups stew)

4½ cups quartered shiitake mushrooms (about 8 ounces)

4½ cups quartered cremini mushrooms (about 8 ounces)

1 (8-ounce) package button mushrooms, quartered

1½ tablespoons olive oil, divided

2 cups thinly sliced leek (about 2 medium)

1 cup chopped fennel bulb (about 1 small bulb)

1 cup (1-inch-thick) slices carrot

¼ teaspoon salt, divided

2 cups Mushroom Stock

1½ tablespoons lower-sodium soy sauce

1 teaspoon minced fresh or ¼ teaspoon dried tarragon

1 teaspoon chopped fresh or ¼ teaspoon dried thyme

1 teaspoon chopped fresh or ¼ teaspoon dried sage

1 teaspoon honey

⅛ teaspoon black pepper

1 (14.5-ounce) can no-salt-added chopped tomatoes, undrained

1 tablespoon cornstarch

1 tablespoon water

2 tablespoons chopped fresh flat-leaf parsley

1 teaspoon grated lemon rind

1 garlic clove, minced

1. Preheat oven to 450°.

2. Combine mushrooms and 1 tablespoon oil in a single layer on a jelly-roll pan. Bake mushrooms at 450° for 30 minutes, stirring once.

3. Heat 1½ teaspoons oil in a Dutch oven over medium heat. Add leek, fennel, and carrot; cook 5 minutes. Sprinkle leek mixture with ⅛ teaspoon salt. Cover, reduce heat, and cook 10 minutes. Uncover; add mushroom mixture, stock, and next 7 ingredients (through tomatoes). Bring to a boil. Reduce heat; simmer 5 minutes. Stir in remaining ⅛ teaspoon salt. Combine cornstarch and water. Stir cornstarch mixture into mushroom mixture, and cook 1 minute.

4. Combine parsley, lemon zest, and garlic. Serve gremolata with stew.

Calories 338; Fat 14g (sat 2g, mono 9.8g, poly 2g); Protein 10.2g; Carb 44.6g; Fiber 7.6g; Chol 0mg; Iron 4.1mg; Sodium 656mg; Calc 137mg

Mushroom Stock

This recipe is used in the Wild Mushroom Stew with Gremolata on page 102.

Yield: 2 cups (serving size: 1 cup stew)

5 cups water

1 cup dried porcini mushrooms
(about 1 ounce)

½ cup chopped celery

⅓ cup dry red wine

¼ cup dried lentils

2 thyme sprigs

1 sage sprig

1 whole garlic head, halved

1. Combine all ingredients in a large saucepan; bring to a boil. Reduce heat, and simmer until reduced to 2 cups (about 40 minutes). Strain stock through a sieve into a bowl; discard solids.

Calories 29; Fat 0.1g (sat 0.0g, mono 0.0g, poly 0.1g); Protein 1.8g; Carb 5.1g; Fiber 1.3g; Chol 0mg; Iron 0.7mg; Sodium 5mg; Calc 18mg

NUTRITION TIP

Unlike most other vegetables, mushrooms contain two important B vitamins—niacin and riboflavin. The shiitake is a particularly healthful mushroom, as it contains lentinan, which may help fight cancer and bolster the immune system.

Creole Shrimp and Sausage Stew

The flavor of the sausage in this recipe will permeate the entire dish, even with the short cooking time.

Yield: 4 servings (serving size: about 1 cup stew)

2 teaspoons olive oil

1 cup chopped green bell pepper

1 cup thinly sliced turkey smoked sausage (about 6 ounces)

1 teaspoon bottled minced garlic

¾ cup fat-free, lower-sodium chicken broth

1 (10-ounce) can diced tomatoes and green chiles, undrained

8 ounces peeled and deveined medium shrimp

1 (15-ounce) can organic kidney beans, rinsed and drained

2 tablespoons chopped fresh parsley

1. Heat a large saucepan over medium-high heat. Add oil to pan; swirl to coat. Add bell pepper, sausage, and garlic to pan; sauté 3 minutes or until bell pepper is tender, stirring occasionally. Add broth and tomatoes; bring to a boil. Stir in shrimp and beans; cover, reduce heat, and simmer 6 minutes or until shrimp are done. Sprinkle with parsley.

Calories 191; Fat 6g (sat 1.7g, mono 2.7g, poly 1g); Protein 21.3g; Carb 13.2g; Fiber 3.5g; Chol 97mg; Iron 2.9mg; Sodium 694mg; Calc 127mg

Thai-Coconut Bouillabaisse

Be sure to reserve the shells after peeling the shrimp; you'll need them to make the broth. *Bouillabaisse* is a classic Provençal seafood stew.

Yield: 6 servings (serving size: 2 clams, 2 mussels, ⅙ shrimp and fish, ⅔ cup broth mixture)

Cooking spray

1 pound peeled and deveined jumbo shrimp (reserve shells)

1 cup chopped celery, divided

1 cup chopped carrot, divided

1 cup chopped onion, divided

2½ cups cold water

3 black peppercorns

1 bay leaf

1 teaspoon olive oil

1 cup chopped red bell pepper

½ cup chopped tomato

1 tablespoon minced fresh garlic

1 teaspoon red curry paste

4 (2 x ½-inch) lime rind strips

1 (13.5-ounce) can light coconut milk

12 littleneck clams, scrubbed

12 mussels, scrubbed and debearded

¼ cup chopped fresh basil

¼ cup chopped fresh cilantro

1 teaspoon salt

¼ teaspoon black pepper

1 (6-ounce) skinless halibut fillet or other lean white fish fillet, cut into 1-inch pieces

Lime wedges (optional)

1. Heat a medium saucepan over medium heat. Coat pan with cooking spray. Add shrimp shells to pan; cook 3 minutes, stirring frequently. Add ½ cup celery, ½ cup carrot, and ½ cup onion to pan; cook 1 minute, stirring occasionally. Stir in 2½ cups cold water, peppercorns, and bay leaf; bring to a boil. Reduce heat, and simmer 30 minutes, stirring occasionally. Strain mixture through a sieve over a bowl; discard solids.

2. Heat oil in a large saucepan over medium heat. Add remaining ½ cup celery, ½ cup carrot, and ½ cup onion to pan; cook 3 minutes, stirring occasionally. Add bell pepper; cook 1 minute, stirring occasionally. Stir in tomato, garlic, curry paste, and rind; cook 2 minutes, stirring frequently. Stir in broth mixture and coconut milk; bring to a boil. Add clams and mussels. Cover, reduce heat, and cook 2 minutes or until clams and mussels open. Remove from heat; discard any unopened shells. Stir in shrimp, basil, and remaining ingredients except lime wedges. Cover and let stand 5 minutes or until shrimp and halibut are done. Discard lime rind. Place 2 clams and 2 mussels in each of 6 bowls. Divide shrimp and fish evenly among bowls. Ladle ⅔ cup broth mixture over each serving. Serve with lime wedges, if desired.

Calories 226; Fat 6.9g (sat 3.5g, mono 1.2g, poly 1.2g); Protein 30.4g; Carb 10.4g; Fiber 1.4g; Chol 143mg; Iron 8mg; Sodium 599mg; Calc 96mg

WINE TIP

In the south of France, bouillabaisse is traditionally served with a dry rosé, a great choice even with this not-so-traditional version. The kick of the red curry paste and cilantro, plus the exotic thick creaminess of the coconut milk, need a refreshing wine that has more weight and power than a white. Try any number of dry rosés from California.

Cioppino-Style Seafood Stew

Inspired by the famous San Francisco meal-in-a-bowl, this comes together with minimal fuss. Serve it with Parmesan toast.

Yield: 4 servings (serving size: 2 cups stew)

1½ tablespoons olive oil

½ cup prechopped onion

1½ teaspoons bottled minced garlic

¼ teaspoon crushed red pepper

1 pound mussels, scrubbed and debearded

8 ounces sea scallops

8 ounces medium shrimp, peeled and deveined

½ cup clam juice

¼ cup chopped fresh flat-leaf parsley

1 (14.5-ounce) can diced tomatoes, undrained

1. Heat olive oil in a Dutch oven over medium-high heat. Add onion, garlic, and red pepper to pan; sauté 2 minutes. Add mussels, scallops, and shrimp to pan; sauté 1 minute. Stir in ½ cup clam juice, parsley, and diced tomatoes; bring to a boil. Cover, reduce heat, and simmer 10 minutes or until mussels open. Discard any unopened shells.

Calories 289; Fat 9.3g (sat 1.5g, mono 4.8g, poly 1.7g); Protein 36.2g; Carb 13.8g; Fiber 1.5g; Chol 138mg; Iron 6.4mg; Sodium 726mg; Calc 88mg

Lobster "Bouillabaisse"

Traditional bouillabaisse uses a variety of fish and shellfish. Enhanced with stock made from lobster shells, this version focuses on the king of crustaceans: lobster. If you'd rather not wrangle live lobsters, ask your fishmonger to steam the lobsters for you (and save the shells). This "bouillabaisse" is also nice (and less costly) with shrimp.

Yield: 8 servings (serving size: ½ lobster tail, ½ cup potato, ¼ cup chopped lobster, and ⅔ cup stock mixture)

5 cups water, divided

2 tablespoons plus ⅛ teaspoon salt, divided

4 (1½-pound) whole Maine lobsters

2 large peeled baking potatoes, cut into ¼-inch cubes (about 1⅓ pounds)

7 cups Shellfish Stock (page 15)

1 cup white wine

3 tablespoons tomato paste

⅛ teaspoon freshly ground black pepper

2 tablespoons minced fresh tarragon

Freshly ground black pepper

1. Bring 4 cups water and 2 tablespoons salt to a boil in a 5-gallon stockpot. Place a vegetable steamer or rack in the bottom of the pot. Add lobsters; steam, covered, 14 minutes or until done. Remove meat from cooked lobster claws. Cut each lobster tail in half, lengthwise; chill meat and tails.

2. Place potatoes in a saucepan; cover with water. Bring to a boil; cook 5 minutes or until tender. Drain; set aside.

3. Preheat oven to 300°.

4. Combine remaining 1 cup water, stock, wine, and tomato paste in a large saucepan; bring to a boil. Cook over medium-high heat 30 minutes or until reduced to 5 cups. Stir in remaining ⅛ teaspoon salt and pepper.

5. While stock reduces, place lobster and potato in a single layer on a baking sheet, keeping separate. Bake at 300° for 20 minutes or until thoroughly heated. Place half a lobster tail in each of 8 shallow soup bowls; place ½ cup potato and ¼ cup chopped lobster in each bowl. Ladle about ⅔ cup stock mixture over each serving; sprinkle each serving with ¾ teaspoon tarragon and black pepper.

Calories 270; Fat 2.6g (sat 0.4g, mono 0.5g, poly 1g); Protein 36.5g; Carb 21g; Fiber 1.8g; Chol 119mg; Iron 2.3mg; Sodium 558mg; Calc 109mg

Southwest Cilantro Fish Stew

Be sure to use Yukon Gold, red potatoes, or another waxy potato in this stew. Russet, Idaho, or other baking potatoes are starchy and can fall apart while cooking.

Yield: 4 servings (serving size: 2½ cups stew)

1 tablespoon olive oil

2 cups chopped onion

1 cup (¼-inch-thick) slices carrot

1 cup (¼-inch-thick) slices celery

3 garlic cloves, minced

1 jalapeño pepper, sliced

4 cups fat-free, lower-sodium chicken broth

2 cups cubed peeled Yukon gold or red potato

1 cup dry white wine

½ cup chopped fresh cilantro

1 (15-ounce) can crushed tomatoes, undrained

1 pound skinless halibut, cut into bite-sized pieces

½ pound peeled and deveined large shrimp

Lime wedges

Cilantro sprigs (optional)

1. Heat oil in a large Dutch oven over medium-high heat. Add onion, carrot, celery, garlic, and jalapeño to pan; sauté 5 minutes or until tender. Stir in broth, potato, wine, cilantro, and tomatoes; bring to a boil. Reduce heat, and simmer 15 minutes or until potato is tender. Add fish and shrimp; cook an additional 5 minutes or until fish and shrimp are done. Ladle 2½ cups stew into each of 4 bowls; serve with lime wedges. Garnish with cilantro sprigs, if desired.

Calories 372; Fat 7.6g (sat 1.2g, mono 3.6g, poly 1.8g); Protein 42.1g; Carb 32.8g; Fiber 5.7g; Chol 122mg; Iron 5.4mg; Sodium 684mg; Calcium 167mg

INGREDIENT TIP

Choose wild-caught Pacific halibut or Alaskan halibut for this recipe; Atlantic halibut has been overfished. If you can't find halibut, Pacific flounder is another good choice.

Mediterranean Fish Stew

Firm-textured halibut stands up to quick simmering and still holds its shape. Serve with crusty French bread and a tossed green salad.

Yield: 4 servings (serving size: 2 cups stew)

1 tablespoon olive oil

½ cup finely chopped onion

2 garlic cloves, minced

2 cups (1-inch) cut green beans (about ½ pound)

⅓ cup thinly sliced carrot

2 (14-ounce) cans fat-free, lower-sodium chicken broth

1 (15-ounce) can cannellini beans or other white beans, rinsed and drained

1 (14.5-ounce) can no-salt-added diced tomatoes, undrained

1 cup uncooked medium seashell pasta

2 tablespoons finely chopped fresh basil

1 tablespoon finely chopped fresh oregano

2 tablespoons tomato paste

¼ teaspoon freshly ground black pepper

¾ pound skinless halibut fillets, cut into 1-inch pieces

¼ cup (1 ounce) shaved Parmesan cheese

1. Heat oil in a Dutch oven over medium-high heat. Add onion and garlic to pan; sauté 5 minutes or until tender. Add green beans and next 4 ingredients (through tomatoes); bring to a boil. Add pasta. Cover, reduce heat, and simmer 12 minutes or until pasta is tender.

2. Stir in basil, oregano, tomato paste, and freshly ground black pepper. Gently stir in fish; cook 3 minutes or until fish flakes easily when tested with a fork or until desired degree of doneness. Sprinkle each serving with Parmesan cheese.

Calories 385; Fat 8.3g (sat 2.1g, mono 4g, poly 1.3g); Protein 31.4g; Carb 45.9g; Fiber 7.9g; Chol 32mg; Iron 4.2mg; Sodium 698mg; Calc 218mg

WINE TIP

The fresh white fruit and subtle berry flavors of a rosé from the Tavel region of France are delicate enough for firm fish, while the generous acidity can handle tomato paste and basil. These dry wines are best when fresh.

Chicken Stew with Sweet Peppers

Try a mix of roasted red, yellow, and orange bell peppers to bring color to this stew.

Yield: 4 servings (serving size: 1½ cups stew)

2 teaspoons olive oil

1 cup finely chopped onion

¾ pound skinless, boneless chicken breast, cut into bite-sized pieces

3 cups chopped zucchini

1 cup finely chopped carrot

⅓ cup canned chopped green chiles, drained

¾ teaspoon dried oregano

½ teaspoon ground cumin

¼ teaspoon salt

¼ teaspoon black pepper

2 garlic cloves, minced

1 (15.5-ounce) can Great Northern beans, drained

1 (14½-ounce) can fat-free, lower-sodium chicken broth

1 cup chopped roasted bell peppers

4 teaspoons chopped fresh cilantro

1. Heat olive oil in a Dutch oven over medium-high heat. Add chopped onion and chicken; sauté 5 minutes or until lightly browned. Add zucchini and next 9 ingredients (through broth); bring to a boil. Cover, reduce heat, and simmer 30 minutes or until vegetables are tender.

2. Add bell peppers, and cook, uncovered, 10 minutes, stirring occasionally. Sprinkle with cilantro.

Calories 262; Fat 4.1g (sat 0.7g, mono 2g, poly 0.7g); Protein 28.3g; Carb 28.8g; Fiber 7.8g; Chol 49mg; Iron 3mg; Sodium 455mg; Calc 96mg

MAKE AHEAD TIP

This stew and the Peruvian Chicken Stew with Sweet Potatoes and Peanuts on the opposite page can be made ahead of time. A nice trick to freshen stew is to add the herbs right before serving, instead of before storing the stew.

Peruvian Chicken Stew with Sweet Potatoes and Peanuts

Cornmeal and potatoes are two of Peru's ancient staples; this recipe incorporates both. We also use a common Peruvian technique: thickening the broth with ground peanuts.

Yield: 6 servings (serving size: 1⅔ cups stew)

½ cup dry-roasted peanuts

1 tablespoon canola oil

1½ cups thinly sliced onion

6 cups water

½ cup yellow cornmeal

1 teaspoon salt

1 teaspoon ground cumin

⅛ teaspoon ground allspice

4 cups julienne-cut peeled sweet potato (about 1 pound)

1½ pounds skinless, boneless chicken breast, cut into bite-sized pieces

¼ cup chopped fresh cilantro

1. Place peanuts in a spice or coffee grinder; process until medium ground.

2. Heat oil in a large Dutch oven over medium-high heat. Add onion; sauté 10 minutes or until lightly browned. Stir in ground peanuts, water, and next 5 ingredients (through sweet potato); bring to a boil. Reduce heat, and simmer 15 minutes. Stir in chicken; cook 10 minutes or until chicken is done. Stir in cilantro.

Calories 347; Fat 10g (sat 1.4g, mono 4.8g, poly 2.9g); Protein 31.9g; Carb 31.8g; Fiber 4.4g; Chol 66mg; Iron 2.1mg; Sodium 504mg; Calc 65mg

Dijon Chicken Stew with Potatoes and Kale

With its dash of Dijon mustard, this stew has a French twist. Serve with some hearty peasant bread.

Yield: 6 servings (serving size: 1½ cups stew)

4 teaspoons olive oil, divided

2 cups sliced leek

4 garlic cloves, minced

1.5 ounces all-purpose flour (about ⅓ cup)

1 pound skinless, boneless chicken thighs, cut into bite-sized pieces

½ pound skinless, boneless chicken breast, cut into bite-sized pieces

½ teaspoon salt, divided

½ teaspoon freshly ground black pepper, divided

1 cup dry white wine

3 cups fat-free, lower-sodium chicken broth, divided

1 tablespoon all-purpose flour

1½ cups water

2 tablespoons Dijon mustard

2 cups (½-inch) cubed peeled white potato (about 1 pound)

8 cups loosely packed torn kale (about 5 ounces)

Crushed red pepper (optional)

1. Heat 1 teaspoon oil in a Dutch oven over medium-high heat. Add leek; sauté 6 minutes or until tender and golden brown. Add garlic; sauté 1 minute. Spoon leek mixture into a large bowl.

2. Place ⅓ cup flour in a shallow bowl or pie plate. Dredge chicken in flour, shaking off excess. Heat remaining 1 tablespoon oil in pan over medium-high heat. Add half of chicken mixture; sprinkle with ⅛ teaspoon salt and ⅛ teaspoon black pepper. Cook 6 minutes, browning on all sides. Add browned chicken to leek mixture. Repeat procedure with remaining chicken mixture, ⅛ teaspoon salt, and ⅛ teaspoon black pepper.

3. Add wine to pan, scraping pan to loosen browned bits. Combine 1 cup broth and 1 tablespoon flour, stirring with a whisk until smooth. Add broth mixture, remaining 2 cups broth, water, and mustard to pan; bring to a boil. Stir in chicken mixture, remaining ¼ teaspoon salt, and remaining ¼ teaspoon black pepper. Cover, reduce heat, and simmer 30 minutes.

4. Stir in potato. Cover and simmer 30 minutes or until potato is tender. Stir in kale; cover and simmer 10 minutes. Garnish with crushed red pepper, if desired.

Calories 324; Fat 7.9g (sat 1.5g, mono 3.5g, poly 1.7g); Protein 30.9g; Carb 33.7g; Fiber 5g; Chol 85mg; Iron 4.6mg; Sodium 659mg; Calc 180mg

Chicken and Okra Stew

Look for okra pods between May and October, and choose pods that are firm, brightly colored, and short. Long okra pods tend to be tough. The "slime" okra is known for will help thicken this stew.

Yield: 6 servings (serving size: 1⅓ cups stew)

4 teaspoons canola oil, divided

2 pounds skinless, boneless chicken thighs, quartered

1 habanero pepper

1½ cups chopped green bell pepper

1 cup finely chopped onion

⅔ cup finely chopped celery

2½ cups chopped plum tomato

2 tablespoons chopped fresh parsley

1 tablespoon chopped fresh oregano

¾ teaspoon salt

1 teaspoon freshly ground black pepper

⅛ teaspoon ground cloves

1 (14-ounce) can fat-free, lower-sodium chicken broth

1 pound fresh okra pods, cut into 1-inch pieces

1. Heat 2 teaspoons oil in a Dutch oven over medium-high heat. Add half of chicken to pan; cook 6 minutes, browning on all sides. Remove chicken from pan. Add remaining chicken to pan; cook 6 minutes, browning on all sides. Remove chicken from pan.

2. Cut habanero in half. Seed one half of pepper, and leave seeds in other half. Mince both pepper halves. Add remaining 2 teaspoons oil to pan; swirl to coat. Add minced habanero, bell pepper, onion, and celery; sauté 5 minutes or until tender, stirring occasionally. Add tomato; cook 3 minutes or until tomato softens. Add parsley and next 5 ingredients (through broth); bring to a boil. Return chicken to pan; cover, reduce heat, and simmer 10 minutes. Add okra; cover and simmer 15 minutes or until okra is just tender.

Calories: 269; Fat 9.4g (sat 1.8g, mono 3.7g, poly 2.5g); Protein 33g; Carb 13.4g; Fiber 4.8g; Chol 126mg; Iron 2.8mg; Sodium 594mg; Calc 106mg

Mexican Turkey Stew

While usually an ingredient in moles, roasted pumpkinseed kernels add another layer of nutty flavor to this posole-style broth. Look for them in specialty markets and health-food stores. Substitute ancho chile powder if guajillo is unavailable.

Yield: 8 servings (serving size: 1⅓ cups stew)

3 large Anaheim chiles, seeded and halved lengthwise

2 teaspoons canola oil

Cooking spray

1½ cups chopped onion

4 garlic cloves, minced

2 tablespoons ground guajillo chile powder

1½ teaspoons dried oregano

4 cups water

3 cups fat-free, lower-sodium chicken broth

1 (15-ounce) can golden or white hominy, drained

4 cups shredded cooked turkey breast

⅓ cup chopped fresh cilantro

¼ teaspoon salt

½ cup roasted unsalted pumpkinseed kernels

½ cup thinly sliced radishes

½ cup thinly sliced green onions

½ cup (2 ounces) crumbled queso fresco cheese

Lime wedges (optional)

Cilantro sprigs (optional)

1. Preheat broiler.

2. Place pepper halves, skin sides up, on a foil-lined baking sheet. Broil 6 minutes or until blackened. Place in a paper bag, and fold to close tightly. Let stand 15 minutes. Peel and chop; set aside.

3. Heat oil in a large Dutch oven coated with cooking spray over medium heat. Add onion to pan; cook 6 minutes, stirring occasionally. Add garlic; cook 1 minute, stirring occasionally. Add chile powder and oregano; cook 1 minute, stirring constantly. Stir in 4 cups water, broth, and hominy; bring to a boil. Reduce heat, and simmer, uncovered, 10 minutes. Stir in Anaheim chiles and turkey; cook 2 minutes. Stir in cilantro and salt; cook 3 minutes. Ladle about 1⅓ cups stew into each of 8 bowls. Top each serving with 1 tablespoon pumpkinseed kernels, 1 tablespoon radishes, 1 tablespoon green onions, and 1 tablespoon cheese. Serve with lime wedges and cilantro sprigs, if desired.

Calories 213; Fat 6.8g (sat 2.3g, mono 1.9g, poly 1.6g); Protein 25.4g; Carb 13.5g; Fiber 3.2g; Chol 56mg; Iron 1.7mg; Sodium 483mg; Calc 88mg

BEER TIP

With Anaheim and guajillo chiles lending their subtle heat, reach for a flavorful chilled beer, like a Scottish-style ale. Look for a beer with a rich, malty sweetness, hinting of caramel, that works to balance the peppery posole. A beer with dark chocolate, toasted nut, and smoky notes complements the roasted pumpkinseeds in this richly layered stew.

Belgian Turkey Ragout

Our recipe is based on the Belgian beef dish carbonnade à la flamande, a thick stew with bacon, beer, onions, and sugar. With turkey instead of beef, it's also like the rich French stew called *ragout*. Purchase 3½ pounds of turkey thighs with skin and bone, or 2¼ pounds of skinless, boneless turkey thighs.

Yield: 8 servings (serving size: 1 cup stew)

3½ pounds turkey thighs

1 teaspoon salt, divided

½ teaspoon black pepper, divided

2 teaspoons olive oil

1 tablespoon butter

4 cups thinly sliced leek (about 5 large)

2 cups (½-inch) pieces carrot

3 tablespoons all-purpose flour

1 cup fat-free, lower-sodium chicken broth

1 tablespoon brown sugar

1 (12-ounce) bottle amber lager

1 tablespoon Dijon mustard

1 tablespoon white wine vinegar

2 tablespoons chopped fresh parsley

1. Preheat oven to 300°.

2. Remove skin from turkey; cut meat from bones. Discard skin and bones; cut meat into 1½-inch pieces. Sprinkle turkey with ½ teaspoon salt and ¼ teaspoon pepper.

3. Heat oil in a small ovenproof Dutch oven over medium-high heat. Add turkey; cook 6 minutes or until browned, stirring occasionally. Remove turkey and juices from pan. Reduce heat to medium; melt butter in pan. Add leek and carrot; cover and cook 12 minutes or until leek begins to brown, stirring occasionally.

4. Return turkey and juices to pan. Sprinkle flour over turkey mixture; stir well to coat. Add remaining ½ teaspoon salt, remaining ¼ teaspoon pepper, broth, sugar, and beer. Bring to a boil; cover. Place in oven. Bake at 300° for 50 minutes or until turkey is tender. Stir in mustard and vinegar; sprinkle with parsley.

Calories 378; Fat 4.4g (sat 1.6g, mono 1.5g, poly 0.7g); Protein 61.5g; Carb 15.8g; Fiber 2.2g; Chol 169mg; Iron 4.6mg; Sodium 526mg; Calc 73mg

Ancho Pork and Hominy Stew

Ancho chile powder is different from chili powder, which is a mix of dried chiles, garlic, and other spices. It is made with only dried poblano chiles and lends a subtle sweetness to this stew.

Yield: 6 servings (serving size: 1⅓ cups stew)

2 tablespoons ancho chile powder

2 teaspoons dried oregano

1½ teaspoons smoked paprika

1 teaspoon ground cumin

½ teaspoon salt

1½ pounds pork tenderloin, trimmed and cut into ½-inch pieces

1 tablespoon olive oil, divided

2 cups chopped onion

1½ cups chopped green bell pepper

1 tablespoon minced garlic

2½ cups fat-free, lower-sodium chicken broth

1 (28-ounce) can hominy, drained

1 (14.5-ounce) can fire-roasted diced tomatoes, undrained

1. Combine first 5 ingredients in a large bowl; set 1½ teaspoons spice mixture aside. Add pork to remaining spice mixture in bowl, tossing well to coat.
2. Heat 2 teaspoons oil in a large Dutch oven over medium-high heat. Add pork mixture to pan; cook 5 minutes or until browned, stirring occasionally. Remove pork from pan; set aside. Add remaining 1 teaspoon oil to pan. Add onion, bell pepper, and garlic; sauté 5 minutes or until tender, stirring occasionally. Return pork to pan. Add reserved 1½ teaspoons spice mixture, broth, hominy, and tomatoes; bring to a boil. Partially cover, reduce heat, and simmer 25 minutes.

Calories 300; Fat 8.3g (sat 2.1g, mono 3.7g, poly 1.4g); Protein 28.9g; Carb 26.9g; Fiber 6.1g; Chol 76mg; Iron 3.2mg; Sodium 523mg; Calc 51mg

Autumn Cranberry Beef Stew

Don't shy away from this stew because of its unusual ingredient—cranberry sauce; it lends a gentle sweet-tart flavor. There's also a nutrition bonus: Cranberries are a good source of vitamins A and C.

Yield: 10 servings (serving size: about ¾ cup stew and ¾ cup noodles)

1 teaspoon dried thyme

½ teaspoon salt

½ teaspoon freshly ground black pepper

1 (3-pound) boneless chuck roast, trimmed and cut into 2-inch cubes

Cooking spray

1 cup chopped onion

1 cup fat-free, lower-sodium beef broth

2 bay leaves

1 (12-ounce) Guinness Stout

1 (10-ounce) package frozen pearl onions, thawed

1 (8-ounce) package button mushrooms, quartered

¼ cup water

2 tablespoons all-purpose flour

¾ cup whole-berry cranberry sauce

8 cups cooked egg noodles (about 1 pound)

Chopped fresh thyme (optional)

1. Combine first 3 ingredients in a small bowl; sprinkle over beef.

2. Heat a Dutch oven over medium-high heat. Coat pan with cooking spray. Add beef to pan; cook 6 minutes, turning to brown on all sides.

3. Add chopped onion, broth, bay leaves, and stout; bring to a boil. Cover, reduce heat, and simmer 2 hours or until beef is tender, stirring occasionally.

4. Stir in pearl onions and mushrooms; cook, covered, 15 minutes, stirring occasionally.

5. Combine ¼ cup water and flour in a small bowl. Add flour mixture and cranberry sauce to pan. Cook 5 minutes. Discard bay leaves. Serve with noodles. Garnish with fresh thyme, if desired.

Calories 479; Fat 14.6g (sat 4.8g, mono 6.3g, poly 1.1g); Protein 39.5g; Carb 43.7g; Fiber 2.6g; Chol 138mg; Iron 6.3mg; Sodium 239mg; Calc 35mg

Hearty Beef and Tomato Stew

You won't have a lot of hands-on time with this stew; the recipe involves mostly measuring and adding ingredients to the pot to simmer. To trim prep time, look for prechopped onions in the produce aisle. Serve with baguette slices.

Yield: 8 servings (serving size: 1½ cups stew)

2 teaspoons olive oil

2 pounds sirloin steak, trimmed and cut into ½-inch cubes

1 cup finely chopped onion (about 1 medium)

3 garlic cloves, minced

1 tablespoon tomato paste

1½ cups fat-free, lower-sodium beef broth

4 cups cubed red potato (1½ pounds)

2 cups sliced carrot

¾ cup pinot noir or other spicy dry red wine

2 teaspoons chopped fresh thyme

1 (16-ounce) package frozen pearl onions

1 (28-ounce) can crushed tomatoes, undrained

1 rosemary sprig

1 bay leaf

1 teaspoon salt

¾ teaspoon freshly ground black pepper

½ cup chopped fresh parsley

1. Heat oil in a large Dutch oven over medium-high heat. Add beef; cook 5 minutes or until browned, stirring frequently. Remove beef from pan, reserving 1 tablespoon drippings in pan. Add onion and garlic to pan; sauté 2 minutes or until onion begins to brown. Add tomato paste; cook 1 minute, stirring frequently. Add broth; bring to a boil. Return meat to pan. Add potato and next 7 ingredients (through bay leaf); bring to a simmer. Cover and cook 1 hour and 15 minutes or until vegetables are tender, stirring occasionally. Discard rosemary and bay leaf. Stir in salt and pepper. Sprinkle with parsley.

Calories 329; Fat 7.5g (sat 2.6g, mono 3.3g, poly 0.4g); Protein 31.1g; Carb 33.3g; Fiber 4.1g; Chol 51mg; Iron 4.3mg; Sodium 630mg; Calc 93mg

NUTRITION TIP

A double-dose of lycopene comes with tomato paste and canned tomatoes: You get 11 milligrams of lycopene per serving—more than twice the amount in a cup of raw tomatoes.

Ropa Vieja

This Cuban stew is made by braising beef until it can be shredded—thus the name *Ropa Vieja* (translated as "old clothes"). Serve with tortillas, and include hot sauce on the side for those who like it fiery. Because the meat is shredded, it's also suitable for tacos and burritos.

Yield: 8 servings (serving size: about ¾ cup stew)

Cooking spray

2 (1-pound) flank steaks, trimmed

3 cups thinly vertically sliced red onion

2 cups red bell pepper strips (about 2 peppers)

2 cups green bell pepper strips (about 2 peppers)

4 garlic cloves, minced

6 tablespoons thinly sliced pitted green olives

1 teaspoon salt

1 teaspoon dried oregano

1 teaspoon ground cumin

½ teaspoon dried rosemary, crushed

½ teaspoon freshly ground black pepper

6 tablespoons sherry vinegar

3 cups fat-free, lower-sodium beef broth

1 tablespoon no-salt-added tomato paste

2 bay leaves

½ cup chopped fresh cilantro

1. Heat a large Dutch oven over medium-high heat. Coat Dutch oven with cooking spray. Add one steak to pan; cook 2½ minutes on each side or until browned. Remove steak from pan. Repeat procedure with cooking spray and remaining steak.

2. Reduce heat to medium. Add onion, bell peppers, and garlic to pan; cook 7 minutes or until tender, stirring frequently. Stir in olives and next 5 ingredients (through black pepper); cook 30 seconds or until fragrant. Stir in vinegar, scraping pan to loosen browned bits; cook 2 minutes or until liquid almost evaporates. Stir in broth, tomato paste, and bay leaves. Add steaks; bring to a simmer. Cover, reduce heat, and cook 1½ hours or until steaks are very tender. Discard bay leaves.

3. Remove steaks from pan; shred with two forks. Stir shredded beef and cilantro into pan.

Calories 229; Fat 9.1g (sat 3.4g, mono 3.9g, poly 0.6g); Protein 26g; Carb 9.6g; Fiber 2g; Chol 40mg; Iron 2.4mg; Sodium 614mg; Calc 53mg

WINE TIP

A savory beef dish such as this needs a rich red wine, but preferably one that won't break the bank since this is a humble meal. Try a blend with zindfandel as the predominant grape.

Fall Stew

This stew is full of vegetables and flavor. You can substitute chuck roast for the lamb in the recipe, if you like. This is a good recipe to use your homemade White Chicken Stock (page 10).

Yield: 4 servings (serving size: 2 cups stew)

2 teaspoons olive oil

¾ pound lean boned leg of lamb or lean, boned chuck roast, cut into 1-inch cubes

1 cup chopped Vidalia or other sweet onion

1 cup chopped celery

¾ cup chopped carrot

3 garlic cloves, minced

½ cup dry red wine

1½ cups cubed baking potato

1 cup chopped peeled rutabaga

1 cup chopped peeled turnip

½ teaspoon salt

7 (10½-ounce) cans fat-free, lower-sodium chicken broth or 8 cups homemade chicken stock

2 bay leaves

½ cup chopped plum tomato

½ cup chopped zucchini

¼ cup chopped fresh cilantro

1 teaspoon dried oregano

1 teaspoon ground cumin

¼ teaspoon ground red pepper

¼ teaspoon black pepper

Cilantro sprigs (optional)

1. Heat oil in a large Dutch oven; add lamb, browning on all sides. Add onion, celery, carrot, and garlic; sauté 5 minutes. Add wine, and cook 3 minutes, stirring frequently.

2. Add potato and next 5 ingredients (through bay leaves); bring to a boil. Reduce heat to medium; cook 1 hour and 20 minutes or until vegetables are tender. Add tomato and remaining ingredients except cilantro sprigs; cook an additional 10 minutes. Discard bay leaves. Garnish with cilantro sprigs, if desired.

Calories 312; Fat 10.2g (sat 2.6g, mono 5.4g, poly 1.4g); Protein 26.3g; Carb 30.7g; Fiber 4.6g; Chol 54mg; Iron 6.2mg; Sodium 595mg; Calc 88mg

Two-Potato Lamb Stew with Roasted Garlic

Roast another head of garlic for making pasta sauces, topping pizzas, spreading onto bread, or stirring into mashed potatoes. Wrap separately in foil, and refrigerate for up to five days.

Yield: 8 servings (serving size: 1⅓ cups stew)

1 whole garlic head

Cooking spray

4 cups coarsely chopped onion

4 garlic cloves, minced

1.5 ounces all-purpose flour (about ⅓ cup)

2 pounds boneless leg of lamb, trimmed and cut into bite-sized pieces

2 teaspoons olive oil

1 teaspoon salt, divided

½ teaspoon freshly ground black pepper, divided

1 cup dry red wine

3 cups fat-free, lower-sodium beef broth

2½ cups (1-inch) cubed peeled sweet potato (about 10 ounces)

2½ cups (1-inch) cubed peeled Yukon gold potato (about 10 ounces)

2½ cups (½-inch) slices peeled parsnip (about 10 ounces)

1 tablespoon chopped fresh rosemary

1. Preheat oven to 350°.

2. Remove white papery skin from garlic head (do not peel or separate the cloves). Wrap garlic head in foil. Bake at 350° for 45 minutes or until tender; cool 10 minutes. Separate cloves; squeeze to extract garlic pulp. Discard skins. Heat a Dutch oven over medium-high heat. Coat pan with cooking spray. Add onion; sauté 10 minutes or until tender and golden brown. Add 4 garlic cloves; sauté 1 minute. Spoon onion mixture into a bowl.

3. Place flour in a shallow bowl or pie plate. Dredge lamb in flour, shaking off excess. Heat oil in pan over medium-high heat. Add half of lamb mixture; sprinkle with ¼ teaspoon salt and ⅛ teaspoon pepper. Cook 6 minutes, browning on all sides. Add browned lamb to onion mixture. Repeat procedure with remaining lamb mixture, ¼ teaspoon salt, and ⅛ teaspoon pepper.

4. Add wine to pan, scraping pan to loosen browned bits. Stir in lamb mixture and broth; bring to a boil. Cover, reduce heat, and simmer 1 hour or until lamb is just tender.

5. Stir in potatoes and parsnip. Cover and simmer 30 minutes. Stir in roasted garlic, remaining ½ teaspoon salt, remaining ¼ teaspoon pepper, and rosemary; simmer 10 minutes.

Calories 316; Fat 10.5g (sat 3.9g, mono 4.8g, poly 0.9g); Protein 20.6g; Carb 35.4g; Fiber 4.9g; Chol 58mg; Iron 2.5mg; Sodium 526mg; Calc 60mg

Duck Stew

For a thicker consistency, coarsely mash one can of beans with a fork or potato masher before adding it to the Dutch oven. Enjoy leftover stew for lunch the next day.

Yield: 6 servings (serving size: about 1⅓ cups stew)

2 teaspoons canola oil

1 pound boneless duck breast halves, skinned and cut into 1-inch pieces

½ pound smoked turkey sausage, sliced

1 cup chopped celery

1 cup chopped carrot

1 cup chopped onion

1½ teaspoons bottled minced garlic

1 cup fat-free, lower-sodium chicken broth

2 (15.8-ounce) cans Great Northern beans, rinsed and drained

1 (14½-ounce) can diced tomatoes, undrained

1. Heat oil in a Dutch oven over medium-high heat. Add duck and sausage; cook 7 minutes or until browned. Remove duck and sausage from pan. Add celery and next 3 ingredients (through garlic); sauté 7 minutes. Return duck mixture to pan. Add broth, beans, and tomatoes; bring to a boil. Reduce heat, and simmer 10 minutes.

Calories 296; Fat 7.8g (sat 2.3g, mono 2.7g, poly 1.5g); Protein 27.5g; Carb 30g; Fiber 8.6g; Chol 71mg; Iron 8.9mg; Sodium 712mg; Calc 107mg

Hungarian Venison Stew

If you can't find venison, this recipe is good with beef stew meat. We found it tasted good with white or red wine. If you prefer less wine flavor, replace some or all the wine with fat-free, lower-sodium beef broth.

Yield: 8 servings (serving size: about ¾ cup stew)

1.1 ounces all-purpose flour (about ¼ cup)

1½ teaspoons salt, divided

½ teaspoon freshly ground black pepper, divided

2 pounds venison, cut into 1-inch cubes

2 tablespoons butter

2 cups chopped onion

2 teaspoons minced garlic

2 cups dry white wine or fruity red wine

2 tablespoons sugar

1 tablespoon sweet Hungarian paprika

1 teaspoon ground red pepper

8 juniper berries

2 whole allspice berries

1 bay leaf

1. Preheat oven to 300°.

2. Lightly spoon flour into a dry measuring cup; level with a knife. Combine flour, ½ teaspoon salt, and ¼ teaspoon black pepper in a large zip-top plastic bag. Add venison; seal and shake to coat. Remove venison from bag; discard remaining flour mixture.

3. Melt butter in an ovenproof Dutch oven over medium-high heat. Add venison, onion, and garlic; sauté 5 minutes, browning venison on all sides. Add wine, scraping pan to loosen browned bits. Add remaining 1 teaspoon salt, remaining ¼ teaspoon black pepper, sugar, and remaining ingredients to pan; bring to a boil.

4. Cover and bake at 300° for 3 hours or until venison is tender. Remove berries and bay leaf before serving.

Calories 212; Fat 5.8g (sat 2.6g, mono 2g, poly 0.8g); Protein 27.1g; Carb 11.9g; Fiber 1.1g; Chol 104mg; Iron 4.6mg; Sodium 527mg; Calc 24mg

INGREDIENT TIP

Pungent allspice and juniper berries lend the stew a spicy, complex flavor; be sure to remove the berries before pouring the stew into a bowl.

chilis

Quick Vegetarian Chili with Avocado Salsa

This colorful chili comes together fast—and the black beans and barley make it a hearty meal.

Yield: 6 servings (serving size: 1 cup soup and 2½ tablespoons avocado salsa)

2 teaspoons canola oil

1 cup chopped onion

1 cup chopped red bell pepper

2 teaspoons chili powder

1 teaspoon ground cumin

1 teaspoon dried oregano

3 garlic cloves, minced

1 (4.5-ounce) can chopped green chiles

⅔ cup uncooked quick-cooking barley

¼ cup water

1 (15-ounce) can no-salt-added black beans, drained

1 (14.5-ounce) can no-salt-added diced tomatoes, undrained

1 (14½-ounce) can organic vegetable broth

4 tablespoons chopped cilantro, divided

½ cup finely chopped peeled avocado

⅓ cup chopped seeded tomato

2 tablespoons finely chopped onion

1 tablespoon finely chopped seeded jalapeño pepper

1 tablespoon fresh lime juice

⅛ teaspoon salt

6 tablespoons reduced-fat sour cream

6 lime wedges

18 baked tortilla chips

1. Heat oil in a Dutch oven over medium-high heat. Add onion and bell pepper; sauté 3 minutes. Add chili powder and next 4 ingredients (through green chiles); cook 1 minute. Stir in barley and next 4 ingredients (through broth); bring to a boil. Cover, reduce heat, and simmer 20 minutes or until barley is tender. Stir in 3 tablespoons cilantro.

2. While the chili simmers, combine remaining 1 tablespoon cilantro, avocado, and next 5 ingredients (through salt); toss mixture gently.

3. Serve chili with avocado salsa mixture, sour cream, lime wedges, and chips.

Note: Store chili in an airtight container in the refrigerator for up to 2 days.

Calories 302; Fat 11g (sat 2.3g, mono 5.9g, poly 1.5g); Protein 8.6g; Carb 46.4g; Fiber 10.4g; Chol 6mg; Iron 2.4mg; Sodium 461mg; Calc 84mg

Hominy Chili with Beans

Hominy is made of dried corn kernels from which the hulls and germs have been removed. You can find it in the canned-vegetable section of the supermarket near the corn.

Yield: 4 servings (serving size: 1¼ cups soup)

2 teaspoons canola oil

2 teaspoons bottled minced garlic

4 teaspoons chili powder

1 teaspoon ground cumin

1 (15.5-ounce) can white hominy, drained

1 (15-ounce) can red beans, drained

1 (14.5-ounce) can no-salt-added diced tomatoes, undrained

1 (14.5-ounce) can no-salt-added stewed tomatoes, undrained and chopped

¼ cup reduced-fat sour cream

¼ cup (1 ounce) shredded reduced-fat sharp cheddar cheese

4 teaspoons minced fresh cilantro

1. Heat oil in a large saucepan over medium heat. Add garlic; sauté 1 minute. Stir in chili powder and next 5 ingredients (through stewed tomatoes); bring to a boil. Reduce heat; simmer, uncovered, 15 minutes. Spoon 1¼ cups chili into each of 4 bowls; top each serving with 1 tablespoon sour cream, 1 tablespoon cheese, and 1 teaspoon cilantro.

Calories 231; Fat 6.4g; (sat 1.9g, mono 2.1g, poly 1.3g); Protein 8.6g; Carb 33.8g; Fiber 8.9g; Chol 8mg; Iron 3.6mg; Sodium 438mg; Calc 143mg

INGREDIENT TIP

If hominy is unavailable, you can substitute 1 (11-ounce) can vacuum-packed white corn or 1 (15.25-ounce) can whole-kernel corn, drained. Hominy imparts a distinctive flavor remarkably different from that of corn, so if you use corn, know that the dish will be more like a basic chili with beans.

Chunky Vegetarian Chili

This vegetarian chili recipe provides a great way for kids to eat fiber-rich foods. It can be taken on camping trips and in school lunches inside an insulated container. (Pictured on page 140.)

Yield: 8 servings (serving size: 1 cup soup)

1 tablespoon vegetable oil

2 cups chopped onion

½ cup chopped yellow bell pepper

½ cup chopped green bell pepper

2 garlic cloves, minced

1 tablespoon brown sugar

1½ tablespoons chili powder

1 teaspoon ground cumin

1 teaspoon dried oregano

½ teaspoon salt

½ teaspoon black pepper

2 (16-ounce) cans stewed tomatoes, undrained

2 (15-ounce) cans no-salt-added black beans, rinsed and drained

1 (15-ounce) can no-salt-added kidney beans, rinsed and drained

1 (15-ounce) can no-salt-added pinto beans, rinsed and drained

1. Heat oil in a Dutch oven over medium-high heat. Add onion, bell peppers, and garlic; sauté 5 minutes or until tender. Add sugar and remaining ingredients, and bring to a boil. Reduce heat, and simmer 30 minutes.

Calories 142; Fat 2.2g (sat 0.3g, mono 0.8g, poly 0.9g); Protein 6.9g; Carb 24.5g; Fiber 8.3g; Chol 0mg; Iron 2.6mg; Sodium 302mg; Calc 87mg

Chicken Green Chili with White Beans

Anaheim chiles have a sweet, bell pepper–like flavor with a bit of mild heat. They are large, 6- to 10-inch-long cone-shaped pods that come in green and red varieties (red ones are also called *chile colorado*). For this recipe, choose peppers with medium to dark green or greenish-red color and no soft spots, bruises, or shriveled skin. Stems should be attached and undamaged.

Yield: 6 servings (serving size: 1½ cups soup)

6 Anaheim chiles

1 tablespoon peanut oil

3 chicken leg quarters, skinned (about 1¾ pounds)

1¾ cups chopped onion

4 garlic cloves, minced

4 cups fat-free, lower-sodium chicken broth

2 cups water, divided

1½ teaspoons ground cumin

1 (15.5-ounce) can no-salt-added cannellini beans or other white beans, rinsed and drained

3 tablespoons all-purpose flour

¾ teaspoon salt

3 tablespoons reduced-fat sour cream

6 lime slices

1. Preheat broiler.

2. Cut chiles in half; discard seeds and membranes. Place halves, skin sides up, on a foil-lined baking sheet; flatten with hand. Broil 5 minutes or until blackened. Place in a heavy-duty zip-top plastic bag; seal. Let stand 15 minutes. Peel chiles; discard skins. Chop chiles.

3. Heat oil in a large Dutch oven over medium-high heat. Add chicken; cook 4 minutes on each side or until browned. Remove chicken from pan. Add onion and garlic, and sauté 6 minutes or until browned, stirring frequently. Return chicken to pan. Add broth, 1½ cups water, and cumin; bring to a simmer. Cook 20 minutes or until chicken is done. Remove chicken; cool slightly. Remove chicken from bones; cut meat into bite-sized pieces. Discard bones. Add chicken to pan; stir in chopped chiles and beans.

4. Combine remaining ½ cup water and flour, stirring with a whisk. Stir into chicken mixture. Bring to a simmer; cook 15 minutes. Stir in salt. Spoon about 1½ cups chili into each of 6 bowls; top each serving with 1½ teaspoons sour cream. Serve with lime slices.

Calories 257; Fat 8.1g (sat 2.1g, mono 2.8g, poly 1.9g); Protein 22.0g; Carb 25.9g; Fiber 5.4g; Chol 48mg; Iron 3.1mg; Sodium 1061mg; Calc 75mg

White Chili

This white chili recipe uses hot pepper sauce made from jalapeños; it's milder than the red hot pepper varieties. Stirring frequently toward the end of cooking time prevents the bean-thickened broth from sticking to the bottom and scorching. Serve with cornbread or Whole Grain Cornsticks (page 254).

Yield: 6 servings (serving size: about ¾ cup soup)

2 teaspoons canola oil

1½ cups chopped onion (about 1 large)

3 garlic cloves, minced

2 cups fat-free, lower-sodium chicken broth

5 teaspoons green hot pepper sauce

½ teaspoon kosher salt

1¼ pounds skinless, boneless chicken breast halves

2 tablespoons stone-ground cornmeal

1 (19-ounce) can cannellini beans or other white beans, rinsed and drained

½ cup plain fat-free yogurt

2 tablespoons thinly sliced green onions (about 1)

Lime wedges (optional)

1. Heat oil in a Dutch oven over medium heat. Add chopped onion and garlic to pan; cook 5 minutes or until onion is tender, stirring occasionally. Add broth, hot pepper sauce, salt, and chicken to pan; bring to a boil. Cover, reduce heat to low, and simmer 15 minutes. Remove chicken from broth mixture; cool.
2. Add cornmeal and beans to broth mixture, stirring with a whisk; simmer 15 minutes. Mash about ¼ cup beans against side of pan. Cut chicken into bite-sized pieces. Add chicken to pan; simmer 5 minutes or until mixture thickens, stirring frequently. Top each serving with yogurt; sprinkle with green onions. Serve with lime wedges, if desired.

Calories 198; Fat 4.1g (sat 0.8g, mono 1.7g, poly 1.2g); Protein 24.8g; Carb 14.3g; Fiber 3g; Chol 56mg; Iron 1.6mg; Sodium 456mg; Calc 63mg

Cincinnati Turkey Chili

Ladle bowlfuls of inspired Midwestern chili for your next casual dinner party or football gathering.

Yield: 4 servings (serving size: about ½ cup spaghetti, 1½ cups soup)

4 ounces uncooked spaghetti

Cooking spray

8 ounces lean ground turkey

1½ cups prechopped onion, divided

1 cup chopped green bell pepper

1 tablespoon bottled minced garlic

1 tablespoon chili powder

2 tablespoons tomato paste

1 teaspoon ground cumin

1 teaspoon dried oregano

¼ teaspoon ground cinnamon

⅛ teaspoon ground allspice

½ cup fat-free, lower-sodium chicken broth

1 (15-ounce) can no-salt-added kidney beans, rinsed and drained

1 (14.5-ounce) can diced tomatoes, undrained

2½ tablespoons chopped semi-sweet chocolate

¼ teaspoon salt

¾ cup (3 ounces) shredded sharp cheddar cheese

1. Cook pasta according to package directions, omitting salt and fat. Drain; set aside.

2. Heat a Dutch oven over medium-high heat. Coat pan with cooking spray. Add turkey; cook 3 minutes, stirring to crumble. Add 1 cup onion, bell pepper, and garlic; sauté 3 minutes. Stir in chili powder and next 5 ingredients (through allspice); cook 1 minute. Add broth, beans, and tomatoes; bring to a boil. Cover, reduce heat, and simmer 20 minutes, stirring occasionally. Remove from heat; stir in chocolate and salt. Serve chili over spaghetti; top evenly with remaining ½ cup onion and cheese.

Calories 428; Fat 15g (sat 7.1g, mono 4.5g, poly 1.6g); Protein 25.1g; Carb 48.9g; Fiber 10g; Chol 67mg; Iron 4.5mg; Sodium 632mg; Calc 236mg

NUTRITION TIP

Not all ground turkey is created equal. Regular ground turkey (labeled 93 percent lean) is a combination of white and dark meat and is fairly high in calories and fat, but it's still leaner than ground round (usually 85 percent lean). Frozen ground turkey, which is all dark meat and may contain skin, can be just as high in fat as ground beef. Ground turkey breast is the lowest in fat, but it can dry out.

Turkey and Bean Chili

With ingredients like prechopped onion and less than 20 minutes cooking time, this flavorful chili comes together very quickly.

Yield: 6 servings (serving size: about 1 cup soup)

1 cup prechopped red onion

⅓ cup chopped seeded poblano pepper (about 1)

1 teaspoon bottled minced garlic

1¼ pounds ground turkey

1 tablespoon chili powder

2 tablespoons tomato paste

2 teaspoons dried oregano

1 teaspoon ground cumin

¼ teaspoon salt

¼ teaspoon black pepper

1 (19-ounce) can cannellini beans, rinsed and drained

1 (14.5-ounce) can diced tomatoes, undrained

1 (14-ounce) can fat-free, lower-sodium chicken broth

½ cup chopped fresh cilantro

6 lime wedges

1. Heat a large saucepan over medium heat. Add first 4 ingredients; cook 6 minutes or until turkey is done, stirring frequently to crumble. Stir in chili powder and next 8 ingredients (through broth); bring to a boil. Reduce heat, and simmer 10 minutes. Stir in cilantro. Serve with lime wedges.

Calories 211; Fat 6.5g (sat 1.7g, mono 1.9g, poly 1.6g); Protein 22.5g; Carb 16.4g; Fiber 4.7g; Chol 54mg; Iron 3.4mg; Sodium 474mg; Calc 52mg

Anasazi and Black Bean Chili

Slightly sweet red-and-white Anasazi beans contrast with robust black beans in flavor and color. You can substitute pintos for the Anasazis, if you prefer.

Yield: 8 servings (serving size: 1½ cups soup)

1¼ cups dried Anasazi beans (about ½ pound)

1¼ cups dried black (turtle) beans (about ½ pound)

Cooking spray

2 cups chopped onion

1 cup chopped red bell pepper

1 cup chopped green bell pepper

½ cup chopped poblano pepper

2 teaspoons minced seeded serrano chile

4 garlic cloves, minced

2 cups fat-free, lower-sodium chicken broth

1 tablespoon ground cumin

1 tablespoon chili powder

2 teaspoons dried oregano

¼ teaspoon ground allspice

3 (14.5-ounce) cans diced tomatoes, undrained

1⅓ cups chopped Spanish chorizo sausage (about 2 links)

Reduced-fat sour cream (optional)

Chopped onion (optional)

1. Sort and wash Anasazi beans; place in a large bowl. Cover with water to 2 inches above beans. Repeat procedure with black beans. Cover and let stand 8 hours or overnight. Drain separately.

2. Place Anasazi beans in a large saucepan; cover with water to 3 inches above beans. Bring to a boil. Reduce heat; simmer 50 minutes or until tender. Drain. Repeat procedure with black beans.

3. Heat a large Dutch oven over medium-high heat. Coat pan with cooking spray. Add onion and next 5 ingredients (through garlic); sauté 6 minutes or until tender. Add beans, broth, and next 5 ingredients (through tomatoes); bring to a boil. Cover, reduce heat, and simmer 15 minutes. Stir in chorizo; simmer 15 minutes. Serve with sour cream and chopped onion, if desired.

Calories 367; Fat 9.9g (sat 3.4g, mono 4.3g, poly 0.9g); Protein 19.4g; Carb 52.2g; Fiber 15.6g; Chol 20mg; Iron 7.3mg; Sodium 635mg; Calc 277mg

BEER TIP

Mexican dark lager offers a heartiness that makes it ideal with chili. Try one that has chocolate flavors, which are perfect with smoky beans, and a touch of caramel sweetness to provide a balance for spicy sausage and chiles.

Pork and Hominy Chili

Mix canned hominy—a nutty, tender ingredient made from dried, hulled corn kernels—with chunks of pork and bold spices in this hearty, Mexican-inspired chili.

Yield: 4 servings (serving size: about 1½ cups soup)

2 teaspoons canola oil

8 ounces boneless center-cut pork chops, trimmed and cubed

1 cup chopped onion (about 1 medium)

¾ cup chopped green bell pepper

2 teaspoons bottled minced garlic

1 tablespoon chili powder

2 teaspoons ground cumin

¼ teaspoon salt

¼ teaspoon freshly ground black pepper

⅛ teaspoon ground red pepper

¼ cup no-salt-added tomato paste

1 (15.5-ounce) can golden hominy, rinsed and drained

1 (14.5-ounce) can no-salt-added diced tomatoes, undrained

1 (14-ounce) can fat-free, lower-sodium chicken broth

¼ cup reduced-fat sour cream

1. Heat oil in a large saucepan over medium-high heat. Add pork to pan; sauté 5 minutes or until lightly browned. Add onion, bell pepper, and garlic to pan; sauté 5 minutes or until tender. Stir in chili powder and next 4 ingredients (through red pepper). Cook 1 minute, stirring constantly. Stir in tomato paste, hominy, tomatoes, and broth; bring to a boil. Reduce heat, and simmer 10 minutes. Serve with sour cream.

Calories 238; Fat 7.8g (sat 2.5g, mono 3g, poly 1.3g); Protein 17.6g; Carb 24.6g; Fiber 5.2g; Chol 33mg; Iron 2.1mg; Sodium 650mg; Calc 61mg

Smoky Slow-Cooker Chili

This chili uses ground pork, diced pork shoulder, and a ham hock for a hearty, smoky flavor that's perfect for cold days. If you don't have a slow cooker, see the tip below for preparing this chili on the stove top.

Yield: 8 servings (serving size: about 1⅓ cups soup)

Cooking spray

1 pound ground pork

1 pound boneless pork shoulder, cut into ½-inch pieces

3 cups chopped onion

1¾ cups chopped green bell pepper

3 garlic cloves, minced

3 tablespoons tomato paste

1 cup lager-style beer

3 tablespoons chili powder

1 tablespoon ground cumin

2 teaspoons dried oregano

¾ teaspoon freshly ground black pepper

6 tomatillos, quartered

2 bay leaves

2 (14½-ounce) cans plum tomatoes, undrained and chopped

1 (15-ounce) can no-salt-added pinto beans, drained

1 (7¾-ounce) can Mexican hot-style tomato sauce

1 smoked ham hock (about 8 ounces)

1½ tablespoons sugar

½ cup finely chopped cilantro

½ cup finely chopped green onions

½ cup (2 ounces) crumbled queso fresco

8 lime wedges

1. Heat a large nonstick skillet over medium-high heat. Coat pan with cooking spray. Add ground pork to pan; cook 5 minutes or until browned, stirring to slightly crumble. Drain well. Transfer pork to an electric slow cooker.
2. Recoat pan with cooking spray. Add pork shoulder; cook 5 minutes or until lightly browned, turning occasionally. Transfer pork to slow cooker.
3. Recoat pan with cooking spray. Add onion and bell pepper; sauté 8 minutes, stirring frequently. Add garlic; sauté 1 minute. Add tomato paste; cook 1 minute, stirring constantly. Stir in beer; cook 1 minute. Transfer onion mixture to slow cooker. Add chili powder and next 9 ingredients (through ham hock) to slow cooker. Cover and cook on HIGH 5 hours or until meat is tender. Remove bay leaves and ham hock; discard. Stir in sugar. Ladle about 1⅓ cups chili into each of 8 bowls; top each serving with 1 tablespoon cilantro, 1 tablespoon green onions, and 1 tablespoon cheese. Serve each serving with 1 lime wedge.

Calories 354; Fat 14.2g (sat 5.1g, mono 5.9g, poly 1.4g); Protein 28.5g; Carb 26.4g; Fiber 6.8g; Chol 82mg; Iron 3.8mg; Sodium 497mg; Calc 108mg

PREP TIP

You can also cook the chili in a slow cooker on LOW for 8 hours. For cooking chili on the stovetop, use a total of 12 ounces beer and simmer, covered, for 2½ to 3 hours or until the pork shoulder is tender.

All-American Chili

This traditional American chili is a comforting classic on a wintry night. Like most chilis, this version tastes even better the next day.

Yield: 8 servings (serving size: 1¼ cups soup)

6 ounces hot turkey Italian sausage

2 cups chopped onion

1 cup chopped green bell pepper

8 garlic cloves, minced

1 pound ground sirloin

1 jalapeño pepper, chopped

2 tablespoons chili powder

2 tablespoons brown sugar

1 tablespoon ground cumin

3 tablespoons tomato paste

1 teaspoon dried oregano

½ teaspoon freshly ground black pepper

¼ teaspoon salt

2 bay leaves

1¼ cups merlot or other fruity red wine

2 (28-ounce) cans no-salt-added whole tomatoes, undrained and coarsely chopped

2 (15-ounce) cans no-salt-added kidney beans, drained

½ cup (2 ounces) shredded reduced-fat sharp cheddar cheese

1. Heat a large Dutch oven over medium-high heat. Remove casings from sausage. Add sausage, onion, and next 4 ingredients (through jalapeño) to pan; cook 8 minutes or until sausage and beef are browned, stirring to crumble.

2. Add chili powder and next 7 ingredients (through bay leaves), and cook 1 minute, stirring constantly. Stir in wine, tomatoes, and kidney beans; bring to a boil. Cover, reduce heat, and simmer 1 hour, stirring occasionally. Uncover and cook 30 minutes, stirring occasionally. Discard bay leaves. Sprinkle each serving with cheddar cheese.

Calories 286; Fat 7.5g (sat 2.1g, mono 1.1g, poly 0.4g); Protein 22.4g; Carb 28.5g; Fiber 6.5g; Chol 48mg; Iron 5.1mg; Sodium 460mg; Calc 169mg

Ancho, Beef, and Kidney Bean Chili

Instead of using commercial chili powder to flavor this stew, we pureed dried ancho chiles for a customized taste. You can prepare the chile-broth puree up to two days in advance to streamline prep for a busy night.

Yield: 10 servings (serving size: 1⅓ cups soup)

2 tablespoons olive oil, divided

2 cups chopped onion

2 teaspoons ground cumin

6 garlic cloves, minced

2 ounces stemmed dried seeded ancho chiles, torn into 2-inch pieces

4 cups fat-free, lower-sodium beef broth

1 (28-ounce) can diced tomatoes, undrained

2 pounds boneless chuck roast, trimmed and cut into 2-inch cubes

Cooking spray

2½ cups chopped green bell pepper (about 2 large)

6 cups cooked kidney beans

¾ teaspoon salt

½ teaspoon freshly ground black pepper

10 tablespoons reduced-fat sour cream

¼ cup chopped fresh cilantro

Lime wedges (optional)

1. Heat 1 tablespoon olive oil in a large saucepan over medium heat. Add onion to pan; cook 8 minutes or until golden, stirring frequently. Add cumin, garlic, and chiles; cook 3 minutes or until chiles are soft, stirring frequently. Stir in broth and tomatoes; bring to a simmer. Cover, remove from heat, and let stand at room temperature 20 minutes.

2. Place half of chile mixture in a blender. Remove center piece of blender lid (to allow steam to escape); secure blender lid on blender. Place a clean towel over opening in blender lid (to avoid splatters). Blend until smooth. Pour pureed chile mixture into a large bowl. Repeat procedure with remaining chile mixture. Set aside.

3. Heat remaining 1 tablespoon oil in a large Dutch oven over medium-high heat. Add beef to pan; sauté 10 minutes or until browned on all sides. Remove beef from pan. Coat pan with cooking spray. Add bell pepper to pan, and sauté 8 minutes or until browned. Stir in pureed chile mixture and beef; bring to a boil. Cover, reduce heat, and simmer 1 hour or until beef is tender. Add beans; cook 20 minutes. Stir in salt and black pepper. Top with sour cream and cilantro; serve with lime wedges, if desired.

Calories 362; Fat 11.7g (sat 4g, mono 5.2g, poly 1.1g); Protein 28.5g; Carb 37.4g; Fiber 11.7g; Chol 60mg; Iron 6.3mg; Sodium 504mg; Calc 86mg

Beef and Beer Chili

Cook a pot of this flavorful chili in just 40 minutes for a quick weeknight meal that's sure to warm the soul. You can easily double the recipe and freeze extra for later.

Yield: 4 servings (serving size: 1½ cups soup)

1½ cups chopped red onion (about 1 medium)

1 cup chopped red bell pepper (about 1 small)

8 ounces ground beef, extra lean

2 garlic cloves, minced

1½ tablespoons chili powder

2 teaspoons ground cumin

1 teaspoon sugar

½ teaspoon salt

½ teaspoon dried oregano

1 (19-ounce) can no-salt-added red kidney beans, drained

1 (14.5-ounce) can no-salt-added diced tomatoes, undrained

1 (14-ounce) can fat-free, lower-sodium beef broth

1 (12-ounce) bottle beer

1 tablespoon yellow cornmeal

1 tablespoon fresh lime juice

1. Combine first 4 ingredients in a large Dutch oven over medium-high heat. Cook 5 minutes or until beef is browned, stirring to crumble. Stir in chili powder, cumin, sugar, and salt; cook 1 minute. Add oregano and next 4 ingredients (through beer) to pan; bring to a boil. Reduce heat, and simmer 15 minutes. Stir in cornmeal; cook 5 minutes. Stir in juice.

Calories 232; Fat 3.3g (sat 0.8g, mono 1g, poly 0.3g); Protein18.2g; Carb 27.2g; Fiber 6.6g; Chol 30mg; Iron 3mg; Sodium 592mg; Calc 69mg

Chili con Carne with Beans

Serve over rice or with Corn Bread Bites (page 257).

Yield: 4 servings (serving size: 1½ cups soup)

1 cup chopped onion

4 teaspoons chili powder

1 tablespoon ground cumin

1 teaspoon bottled minced garlic

¼ teaspoon ground red pepper

1 pound ground sirloin

1½ cups canned crushed tomatoes

¼ teaspoon salt

1 (14.5-ounce) can diced tomatoes with green pepper, celery, and onion

1 (19-ounce) can no-salt-added kidney beans, rinsed and drained

1. Cook first 6 ingredients in a large nonstick skillet over medium-high heat until beef is browned, stirring to crumble. Add crushed tomatoes, salt, and diced tomatoes; bring to a boil. Reduce heat and simmer 4 minutes, stirring occasionally. Add beans; cook 2 minutes or until thoroughly heated.

Calories 304; Fat 6.2g (sat 2.1g, mono 2.1g, poly 0.8g); Protein 31.1g; Carb 34.2g; Fiber 12.7g; Chol 60mg; Iron 5.6mg; Sodium 589mg; Calc 131mg

INGREDIENT TIP

Unlike pure "chile" powder made with ground dried chile peppers, "chili" powder typically contains a blend of seasonings such as cumin, paprika, garlic, and salt along with ground chiles. In 1892, German immigrant and Texas saloon owner William Gebhardt figured out a way to preserve his fall chile harvest by running them through a meat grinder, and then drying and pulverizing them. He was later inspired to add cumin, oregano, and black pepper to the mix.

Easy Elk Chili

Substitute ground venison, buffalo, or lean beef for the elk. You can prepare this chili up to a day ahead, cool to room temperature, and refrigerate. Freeze leftovers in individual freezer-safe zip-top plastic bags for up to two months.

Yield: 6 servings (serving size: about 1 cup soup)

1 pound ground elk

2 cups chopped yellow onion

1 cup dry red wine

1½ cups water

1 tablespoon chipotle chile powder

2 teaspoons ground cumin

2 teaspoons dried oregano

½ teaspoon salt

2 (14.5-ounce) cans diced tomatoes, undrained

2 (14-ounce) cans fat-free, lower-sodium beef broth

1 (15-ounce) can red kidney beans, rinsed and drained

¼ cup reduced-fat sour cream

¼ cup (1 ounce) reduced-fat shredded cheddar cheese

2 tablespoons chopped green onions

1. Combine elk and 2 cups onion in a Dutch oven; cook over medium-high heat until lightly browned, stirring to crumble. Add wine; bring to a boil. Cook 3 minutes. Stir in 1½ cups water, chipotle chile powder, and next 6 ingredients (through beans); bring to a boil. Partially cover, reduce heat, and simmer 2 hours (add more water if mixture becomes too thick). Ladle about 1 cup chili into each of 6 bowls; spoon 2 teaspoons sour cream over each. Sprinkle each with 2 teaspoons cheese and 1 teaspoon green onions.

Calories 282; Fat 7.8g (sat 3.8g, mono 2.1g, poly 0.5g); Protein 23g; Carb 24.3g; Fiber 7.9g; Chol 51mg; Iron 3.3mg; Sodium 685mg; Calc 106mg

Venison Chili

Many New Englanders have freezers stocked with venison from hunting expeditions. If venison is not available, substitute ground sirloin. Garnish with reduced-fat sour cream and/or reduced-fat shredded cheddar, if desired. You can make the chili a day ahead and refrigerate; reheat in the microwave or on the stovetop.

Yield: 4 servings (serving size: 1½ cups soup)

Cooking spray

1 pound ground venison

1 cup chopped sweet onion

1 cup chopped green bell pepper

4 garlic cloves, minced

1 jalapeño pepper, seeded and chopped

2 tablespoons chili powder

¼ teaspoon salt

½ teaspoon ground cumin

½ teaspoon ground red pepper

½ teaspoon freshly ground black pepper

1 (14.5-ounce) can diced tomatoes, undrained

1 (14-ounce) can fat-free, lower-sodium chicken broth

1 tablespoon no-salt-added tomato paste

1 (15-ounce) can no-salt-added red kidney beans, rinsed and drained

1. Heat a small Dutch oven over medium-high heat. Coat pan with cooking spray. Add venison; cook 3 minutes or until browned, stirring to crumble. Remove from pan with a slotted spoon. Cover and keep warm.

2. Reduce heat to medium. Add onion, bell pepper, garlic, and jalapeño to pan; cook 10 minutes or until tender, stirring frequently. Stir in chili powder and next 4 ingredients (through black pepper). Add venison, diced tomatoes, broth, and tomato paste, stirring until well combined; bring to a boil. Cover; reduce heat, and simmer 30 minutes. Add red kidney beans; cook, uncovered, 15 minutes.

Calories 262; Fat 4g (sat 1.3g, mono 1g, poly 0.9g); Protein 33.3g; Carb 23.5g; Fiber 9g; Chol 96mg; Iron 6.4mg; Sodium 643mg; Calc 86mg

chowders & bisques

Grilled Corn and Potato Chowder

Grilling the corn helps to bring out its natural sweetness, as well as adding a slight smokiness to this chowder.

Yield: 6 servings (serving size: 1 cup soup)

1 pound small red potatoes, quartered

1 tablespoon salt, divided

3 tablespoons softened butter, divided

4 ears shucked corn

Cooking spray

¾ cup finely chopped onion

⅛ teaspoon ground red pepper

3 cups 2% reduced-fat milk

½ cup half-and-half

2 thyme sprigs

3 tablespoons finely chopped chives

1½ teaspoons chopped fresh thyme

½ teaspoon freshly ground black pepper

1. Preheat grill to medium-high heat.

2. Place a grill basket on grill.

3. Place potatoes and 2 teaspoons salt in a saucepan; cover with water. Bring to a boil; cook 2 minutes. Remove from heat. Let potatoes stand in hot water 5 minutes. Drain; cut into ¼-inch cubes.

4. Melt 1 tablespoon butter; brush evenly over corn. Place corn on grill rack coated with cooking spray. Place potatoes in grill basket coated with cooking spray. Grill corn and potatoes 15 minutes or until slightly charred, turning occasionally. Cool corn slightly; cut kernels from cobs. Place 1 cup corn kernels in a food processor; process until smooth.

5. Melt remaining 2 tablespoons butter in a medium saucepan over medium-high heat. Add onion; sauté 3 minutes, stirring occasionally. Add remaining 1 teaspoon salt and red pepper; cook 30 seconds, stirring frequently. Stir in potatoes, remaining corn kernels, pureed corn, milk, half-and-half, and thyme sprigs; bring to a simmer. Reduce heat; simmer 20 minutes, stirring occasionally. Discard thyme sprigs. Stir in chives and remaining ingredients.

Calories 268; Fat 12.3g (sat 6.6g, mono 2.2g, poly 0.4g); Protein 9.9g; Carb 33.8g; Fiber 3.1g; Chol 32mg; Iron 1mg; Sodium 599mg; Calc 214mg

WINE TIP

This corn chowder calls for a smooth, full-bodied white, like a French chardonnay. Chardonnay's buttery nuance is a perfect match for grilled corn, while the acidity balances the creaminess.

Roasted Corn, Pepper, and Tomato Chowder

Blue cheese provides a pungent counterpoint in this soup. Substitute crumbled goat cheese or feta, if you prefer.

Yield: 6 servings (serving size: 1½ cups soup)

3 red bell peppers, halved and seeded

3 ears shucked corn

1½ pounds tomatoes, halved, seeded, and peeled (about 4)

2 tablespoons extra-virgin olive oil

4 cups chopped onion (about 2 medium)

3 (14-ounce) cans fat-free, lower-sodium chicken broth

¼ teaspoon salt

¼ teaspoon freshly ground black pepper

¼ cup (1 ounce) crumbled blue cheese

2 tablespoons chopped fresh chives

1. Prepare grill to medium-high heat.

2. Arrange bell peppers, skin sides down, and corn in a single layer on grill rack; grill 5 minutes, turning corn occasionally. Add tomatoes; grill an additional 5 minutes or until vegetables are slightly charred. Remove from heat; cool 10 minutes. Coarsely chop tomatoes and bell peppers; place in a medium bowl. Cut kernels from ears of corn; add to tomato mixture.

3. Heat oil in a large Dutch oven over medium heat. Add onion; cook 7 minutes or until tender, stirring occasionally. Stir in tomato mixture; cook 3 minutes, stirring occasionally. Increase heat to high, and stir in broth. Bring to a boil. Reduce heat, and simmer 30 minutes or until vegetables are tender. Cool 20 minutes.

4. Place one-third of tomato mixture in a blender; process until smooth. Place pureed mixture in a large bowl. Repeat procedure twice with remaining tomato mixture. Wipe pan clean with paper towels. Press tomato mixture through a sieve into pan; discard solids. Place pan over medium heat; cook until thoroughly heated. Stir in salt and black pepper. Ladle about 1½ cups chowder into each of 6 bowls; top each serving with 2 teaspoons cheese and 1 teaspoon chives.

Calories 155; Fat 7.2g (sat 1.7g, mono 3.9g, poly 1.2g); Protein 5.4g; Carb 21g; Fiber 4.4g; Chol 4mg; Iron 1.1mg; Sodium 620mg; Calc 45mg

Cauliflower and Red-Pepper Chowder

This chowder tastes best after it's chilled for a few hours and the flavors have had a chance to meld. Leaving a portion of the soup chunky gives the finished product a hearty consistency. Serve with breadsticks or with a homemade Baguette (page 242).

Yield: 5 servings (serving size: 2 cups soup)

1 tablespoon butter

⅔ cup minced shallots (about 4 large)

½ cup sliced celery

2 (14½-ounce) cans organic vegetable broth

1½ cups water

6 cups finely chopped cauliflower florets (about 1 head)

2 cups finely chopped red bell pepper (about 2 medium)

1 cup finely chopped peeled red potato

1 bay leaf

1 cup 2% reduced-fat milk

½ teaspoon black pepper

3 tablespoons minced fresh or 1 tablespoon dried basil

5 tablespoons reduced-fat sour cream

1. Melt butter in a Dutch oven over medium heat. Add shallots and celery; cook 5 minutes, stirring constantly. Add broth and water; bring to a boil. Add cauliflower, bell pepper, potato, and bay leaf; return to a boil. Reduce heat, and simmer 20 minutes or until potato is tender. Stir in milk and black pepper. Cool slightly; discard bay leaf.

2. Place 1½ cups soup in a blender or food processor; process until smooth. Pour pureed soup into a large bowl. Repeat procedure with an additional 1½ cups soup. Add remaining soup to the pureed soup, and stir in basil. Return soup to pan, and bring to a boil over medium-high heat, stirring frequently. Remove from heat. Spoon 2 cups chowder into each of 5 bowls; top each serving with 1 tablespoon sour cream.

Calories 83; Fat 2.8g (sat 1.7g, mono 0.5g, poly 0.1g); Protein 3.3g; Carb 12.2g; Fiber 2.5g; Chol 9mg; Iron 0.7mg; Sodium 256mg; Calc 67mg

INGREDIENT TIP

Dried herbs can often work as well as fresh in stews, braises, pasta sauces, or in chowders like this, where they simmer for a while and their intensity has a chance to soften.

Chunky Potato-and-Swiss Chowder

Used with balance and moderation, even half-and-half is fine for healthy eating. A little goes a long way in this rich-tasting soup that's a meal in itself.

Yield: 5 servings (serving size: 1½ cups soup)

Cooking spray

2 cups thinly sliced leek (about 2 large)

2 garlic cloves, minced

4 cups cubed peeled Yukon gold potato (about 1½ pounds)

1 cup cubed carrot (about ½ pound)

1 cup cubed yellow squash

2 (15.75-ounce) cans fat-free, lower-sodium chicken broth

2 bay leaves

1 cup hot cooked wild rice

1 cup half-and-half

½ cup (2 ounces) shredded Swiss cheese

½ teaspoon salt

¼ teaspoon black pepper

Chopped fresh parsley (optional)

1. Heat a large Dutch oven over medium-high heat. Coat pan with cooking spray. Add leek and garlic; sauté 3 minutes or until tender. Stir in potato and next 4 ingredients (through bay leaves); bring to a boil. Cover, reduce heat, and simmer 20 minutes or until tender. Discard bay leaves. Place half of potato mixture in a blender. Remove center piece of blender lid (to allow steam to escape); secure lid on blender. Place a clean towel over opening in lid (to avoid splatters). Process until smooth. Return pureed potato mixture to pan; stir in rice and remaining ingredients except parsley. Cook over medium heat until cheese melts. Sprinkle with parsley, if desired.

Calories 302; Fat 9.5g (sat 5.6g, mono 2.6g, poly 0.8g); Protein 12.4g; Carb 43g; Fiber 4.2g; Chol 28mg; Iron 2.3mg; Sodium 693mg; Calc 209mg

Curried Squash-and-Pear Bisque

Curry powder adds a spicy note that rounds out the sweetness from the pear and squash in this warming soup.

Yield: 8 servings (serving size: 1¼ cups soup)

1 butternut squash (about 2¾ pounds)

1 tablespoon butter

2 cups chopped peeled Bartlett pear (about 1 pound)

1½ cups thinly sliced onion

2⅓ cups water

1 cup pear nectar

2 (14½-ounce) cans organic vegetable broth

2½ teaspoons curry powder

⅛ teaspoon salt

⅛ teaspoon black pepper

½ cup half-and-half

1 small Bartlett pear, cored and thinly sliced

Dash black pepper (optional)

1. Preheat oven to 375°.

2. Cut squash in half lengthwise; discard seeds and membrane. Place squash halves, cut sides down, on a baking sheet; bake at 375° for 45 minutes or until tender. Cool. Peel squash; mash pulp. Set aside 3½ cups pulp, reserving remaining squash for another use.

3. Melt butter in a large Dutch oven over medium-high heat. Add chopped pear and onion; sauté 10 minutes or until lightly browned. Add squash pulp, water, and next 5 ingredients (through pepper). Bring to a boil; partially cover, reduce heat, and simmer 40 minutes. Place one-third of squash mixture in a blender. Remove center piece of blender lid (to allow steam to escape); secure lid on blender. Place a clean towel over opening in lid (to avoid splatters). Process until smooth. Pour pureed mixture into a large bowl; repeat procedure with remaining squash mixture. Return squash mixture to pan; stir in half-and-half. Cook over low heat 3 minutes or until thoroughly heated. Ladle bisque into bowls, and garnish with pear slices and black pepper, if desired.

Calories 165; Fat 3.5g (sat 2g, mono 0.4g, poly 0.2g); Protein 2.3g; Carb 34.9g; Fiber 7.1g; Chol 10mg; Iron 1mg; Sodium 322mg; Calc 89mg

Herbed Fish and Red Potato Chowder

If you can't find halibut, substitute cod or another flaky white fish. Serve with bread.

Yield: 4 servings (serving size: 2 cups soup)

2 bacon slices

3 cups diced red potato (about 1 pound)

1 cup chopped onion

3 tablespoons all-purpose flour

2 (8-ounce) bottles clam juice

2 cups 2% reduced-fat milk

1 tablespoon chopped fresh thyme

¼ teaspoon salt

¼ teaspoon black pepper

12 ounces skinless halibut fillets, cut into 1-inch pieces

2 tablespoons chopped fresh flat-leaf parsley

1. Cook bacon in a Dutch oven over medium-high heat until crisp. Remove bacon from pan. Reserve 1 tablespoon bacon drippings in pan; discard remaining drippings. Cool bacon, and crumble. Set bacon aside.

2. Add potato and onion to drippings in pan; sauté 3 minutes or until onion is tender. Add flour to pan; cook 1 minute, stirring constantly. Stir in clam juice; bring to a boil. Cover, reduce heat, and simmer 6 minutes or until potatoes are tender.

3. Stir in milk; bring to a simmer over medium-high heat, stirring constantly (do not boil). Stir in thyme, salt, pepper, and fish; cook 3 minutes or until desired degree of doneness. Stir in parsley. Sprinkle with reserved bacon.

Calories 307; Fat 8.1g (sat 3.5g, mono 3g, poly 0.9g); Protein 24.4g; Carb 33.9g; Fiber 2.5g; Chol 57mg; Iron 2.2mg; Sodium 611mg; Calc 198mg

Lobster Bisque

Lobster shells flavor the broth in this dish, while potato adds body. Finished with a splash of brandy, this delicious bisque is most satisfying as a first course.

Yield: 12 servings (serving size: ⅔ cup soup)

5 cups water, divided

2 cups clam juice

¾ cup dry white wine, divided

2 (1¼-pound) whole Maine lobsters

1½ cups chopped carrot, divided

1½ cups chopped celery, divided

1½ cups chopped onion, divided

1 cup chopped fennel bulb, divided

1 cup fat-free, lower-sodium chicken broth

1 teaspoon dried tarragon

½ teaspoon dried thyme

5 parsley sprigs

2 bay leaves

1½ tablespoons butter

2 garlic cloves, minced

2 tablespoons all-purpose flour

1 cup chopped peeled baking potato

1 (14.5-ounce) can diced tomatoes, drained

1 cup fat-free milk

¼ cup whipping cream

2 tablespoons brandy

Chive sprigs (optional)

1. Combine 3 cups water, clam juice, and ½ cup wine in an 8-quart stockpot; bring to a boil. Add lobsters; cover and cook 10 minutes or until shells are bright orange-red and tails are curled. Remove lobsters from pan, reserving liquid in pan. Cool lobsters. Remove meat from tail and claws. Discard tomalley and any roe. Chop meat; chill until ready to use. Place lobster shells in pan. Add remaining 2 cups water, 1 cup carrot, 1 cup celery, 1 cup onion, ½ cup fennel, broth, tarragon, thyme, parsley, and bay leaves; bring to a boil. Reduce heat, and simmer, partially covered, 1½ hours. Drain through a fine sieve over a bowl; discard solids.

2. Melt butter in pan over medium heat; add remaining ½ cup carrot, remaining ½ cup celery, remaining ½ cup onion, remaining ½ cup fennel, and garlic; sauté 5 minutes. Add remaining ¼ cup wine; cook 3 minutes or until liquid almost evaporates. Sprinkle flour over carrot mixture; cook 1 minute, stirring constantly. Stir in reserved cooking liquid and potato; cook 20 minutes or until potato is tender. Add tomatoes; cook 10 minutes. Place one-third of mixture in blender. Remove center piece of blender lid (to allow steam to escape); secure lid on blender. Place a clean towel over opening in lid (to avoid splatters). Process until smooth. Pour pureed mixture into a large bowl. Repeat procedure twice with remaining mixture. Return pureed mixture to pan. Stir in reserved lobster, milk, cream, and brandy; cook 5 minutes over medium-low heat or until thoroughly heated (do not boil). Garnish with chive sprigs, if desired.

Calories 153; Fat 4.1g (sat 2g, mono 1.3g, poly 0.3g); Protein 16.3g; Carb 9g; Fiber 1.4g; Chol 84mg; Iron 0.8mg; Sodium 407mg; Calc 83mg

Lobster Chowder

If you're using store-bought lobster meat, you can substitute equal parts clam juice and chicken broth for the lobster stock, which is made from lobster shells. The recipe also works with two pounds of shrimp, substituting shrimp shells for the lobster shells. This chowder tastes best after it's spent an hour or two in the refrigerator, but you can serve it immediately, if you prefer.

Yield: 8 servings (serving size: 1 cup soup)

3 gallons water

¾ cup salt

2 (1½-pound) live Maine lobsters or 2½ cups chopped cooked lobster meat

8 cups water

2 bay leaves

2 bacon slices, chopped

1 cup chopped green onions

1 teaspoon Hungarian sweet paprika

½ teaspoon ground cumin

2 cups diced peeled baking potato

1 cup half-and-half

2 teaspoons sugar

½ teaspoon salt

¼ teaspoon white pepper

2 cups fresh corn kernels (about 4 ears)

Chopped fresh chives (optional)

1. Combine 3 gallons water and ¾ cup salt in a 5-gallon stockpot; bring to a boil. Add lobsters; cover and cook 10 minutes or until shells are bright orange-red and tails are curled. Remove lobsters from pan; cool. Discard cooking liquid. Remove meat from tail and claws. Discard tomalley and any roe. Coarsely chop meat; refrigerate. Reserve shells.

2. Combine lobster shells, 8 cups water, and bay leaves in stockpot. Bring to a boil, reduce heat, and simmer 1 hour. Strain lobster stock through a colander into a large bowl; discard shells and bay leaves. Reserve 4 cups of stock.

3. Cook bacon in a large Dutch oven over medium-high heat until crisp. Add onions; sauté 2 minutes. Stir in paprika and cumin. Add reserved 4 cups stock and potato; bring to a boil. Cook 15 minutes or until potato is tender. Remove from heat. Stir in reserved lobster meat, half-and-half, sugar, ½ teaspoon salt, and pepper. Cover and refrigerate 1 hour, if desired.

4. Return pan to low heat. Add corn; cook 5 minutes. Garnish with chives, if desired.

Calories 204; Fat 7.9g (sat 3.7g, mono 2.8g, poly 0.8g); Protein 13.2g; Carb 21g; Fiber 2.2g; Chol 49mg; Iron 0.9mg; Sodium 385mg; Calc 71mg

INGREDIENT TIP

Wild American lobster is an environmentally friendly seafood choice. Many fish and shrimp are trawled in nets that catch all kinds of things, but lobsters are caught in traps that don't disturb the seafloor.

Thai Shrimp Bisque

The homemade stock adds depth of flavor that is worth the effort. If you're in a rush, use shrimp that has already been shelled and store-bought seafood stock in place of the water and shrimp shells in step 2.

Yield: 6 servings (serving size: 1½ cups soup)

Marinade:

1½ pounds medium shrimp

1½ tablespoons grated lime rind

⅓ cup fresh lime juice

1½ tablespoons ground coriander

1 tablespoon minced fresh cilantro

1 tablespoon minced peeled fresh ginger

1½ teaspoons sugar

¼ teaspoon ground red pepper

2 garlic cloves, crushed

Shrimp stock:

2 cups water

¼ cup dry white wine

1 tablespoon tomato paste

Soup:

1 teaspoon olive oil

½ cup chopped onion

⅓ cup chopped celery

1 (14-ounce) can light coconut milk

1 tablespoon tomato paste

1.1 ounces all-purpose flour
(about ¼ cup)

1 cup 2% reduced-fat milk

1 tablespoon grated lime rind

1 tablespoon minced fresh cilantro

½ teaspoon salt

1. Peel shrimp, reserving shells. Combine shrimp and next 8 ingredients (though garlic) in a large zip-top plastic bag; seal and marinate in refrigerator 30 minutes.

2. Combine reserved shrimp shells, water, wine and tomato paste in a large Dutch oven. Bring to a boil. Reduce heat; simmer until liquid is reduced to 1 cup (about 10 minutes). Strain stock through a sieve over a bowl; discard solids.

3. Heat oil in a large Dutch oven over medium heat. Add onion and celery, and sauté 8 minutes or until browned. Add 1 cup shrimp stock, coconut milk, and 1 tablespoon tomato paste, scraping pan to loosen browned bits. Bring to a boil. Lightly spoon flour into a dry measuring cup; level with a knife. Combine flour and milk in a small bowl, stirring with a whisk. Add to pan; reduce heat, and simmer until thick (about 5 minutes). Add shrimp and marinade, and cook 5 minutes. Stir in lime rind, cilantro, and salt.

Calories 201; Fat 6.7g (sat 3.2g, mono 1.7g, poly 1.2g); Protein 19.9g; Carb 15.2g; Fiber 0.9g; Chol 133mg; Iron 3.3mg; Sodium 380mg; Calc 117mg

Chilled Corn Bisque with Basil, Avocado, and Crab

Allow soup to stand 30 minutes at room temperature before serving; the flavor will come through better if you take off the chill. Chop the basil and the avocado just before topping the bisque so they don't begin to brown.

Yield: 8 servings (serving size: ⅔ cup soup)

3 cups fat-free, lower-sodium chicken broth

3 tablespoons cornstarch

1 tablespoon butter

1 cup finely chopped onion

1 garlic clove, minced

4 cups fresh corn kernels (about 8 ears)

¾ teaspoon salt

¼ teaspoon ground red pepper

½ cup 2% reduced-fat milk

½ cup half-and-half

8 ounces lump crabmeat, shell pieces removed (about 1½ cups)

⅓ cup chopped peeled avocado

3 tablespoons chopped fresh basil

1. Combine broth and cornstarch, stirring with a whisk.

2. Melt butter in a large saucepan over medium-high heat. Add onion; sauté 3 minutes. Add garlic; sauté 30 seconds. Stir in broth mixture, corn, salt, and pepper; bring to a simmer. Cook 10 minutes, stirring frequently (do not boil). Place half of corn mixture in a blender. Remove center piece of blender lid (to allow steam to escape); secure lid on blender. Place a clean towel over opening in lid (to avoid splatters). Process until smooth. Pour pureed corn mixture into a large bowl. Repeat procedure with remaining corn mixture. Strain corn mixture through a sieve into a large bowl; discard solids. Stir in milk and half-and-half; refrigerate two hours or until thoroughly chilled. Before serving, let stand 30 minutes at room temperature; stir well.

3. Ladle ⅔ cup bisque into each of 8 bowls; top each serving with 3 tablespoons crab, about 2 teaspoons avocado, and about 1 teaspoon basil.

Calories 159; Fat 5.3g (sat 2.4g, mono 1.9g, poly 0.7g); Protein 10.8g; Carb 18g; Fiber 2.3g; Chol 34mg; Iron 0.6mg; Sodium 536mg; Calc 64mg

Crab Bisque

Be sure to use a blender instead of a food processor to ensure a perfectly creamy texture in this rich, indulgent bisque.

Yield: 8 servings (serving size: ¾ cup soup and about ¼ cup crabmeat mixture)

Cooking spray

1¼ cups thinly sliced shallots
(about 4 large)

1 celery stalk, finely chopped
(about ½ cup)

4 garlic cloves, minced

3 tablespoons vermouth

¾ teaspoon kosher salt

¼ teaspoon freshly ground black
pepper

⅛ teaspoon ground red pepper

1 pound jumbo lump crabmeat,
shell pieces removed and divided

3 cups fat-free milk

1 cup clam juice

1.5 ounces all-purpose flour
(about ⅓ cup)

½ cup heavy whipping cream

2 tablespoons chopped fresh chives

1½ teaspoons fresh lemon juice

1. Heat a large Dutch oven over medium heat. Coat pan with cooking spray. Add shallots and celery to pan; cook 10 minutes or until softened, stirring occasionally. Add garlic; cook 1 minute. Stir in vermouth; cook 1 minute or until liquid evaporates. Add salt, peppers, and 8 ounces crabmeat.
2. Combine milk and clam juice in a large bowl. Lightly spoon flour into a dry measuring cup; level with a knife. Whisk flour into milk mixture; add to pan. Bring to a boil, stirring constantly. Cook 1 minute or until slightly thickened, stirring constantly.
3. Place half of milk mixture in blender. Remove center piece of blender lid (to allow steam to escape); secure lid on blender. Place a clean towel over opening in lid (to avoid splatters). Blend until smooth. Pour into a large bowl. Repeat procedure with remaining milk mixture. Return pureed mixture to pan. Stir in cream; cook over medium heat 3 minutes or until thoroughly heated.
4. Combine remaining 8 ounces crabmeat, chives, and lemon juice in a medium bowl. Top bisque with crabmeat mixture.

Calories 188; Fat 6.7g (sat 3.6g, mono 1.8g, poly 0.6g); Protein 16.3g; Carb 14.1g; Fiber 0.5g; Chol 80mg; Iron 1.3mg; Sodium 453mg; Calc 204mg

WINE TIP

If there's ever a time to pull out a good chardonnay, it's when crab is on the table. The wine's lush apple fruit enhances the sweet shellfish, and if you pick a wine with an edge of creamy citrus, it works like a twist of lemon.

Scallop Chowder

We liked the flavor of the clam juice in this soup, but you could substitute fat-free, lower-sodium chicken broth. If you don't have Pernod on hand, or prefer to omit the alcohol, substitute one teaspoon anise extract or finely ground aniseed. Serve with crackers.

Yield: 8 servings (serving size: about 1¼ cups soup)

2 teaspoons butter

Cooking spray

1½ cups chopped onion (about 1 medium)

¼ cup chopped celery

1 teaspoon minced garlic

4½ cups (½-inch) cubed peeled Yukon gold or red potato (about 1½ pounds)

½ teaspoon salt, divided

1 teaspoon freshly ground black pepper, divided

1.1 ounces all-purpose flour (about ¼ cup)

2½ cups clam juice

2½ cups 2% reduced-fat milk

1 tablespoon Pernod, licorice-flavored liqueur

1½ teaspoons chopped fresh thyme

1½ pounds sea scallops, cut into 1-inch chunks

1½ cups half-and-half

¼ cup chopped fresh chives

1. Melt 2 teaspoons butter in a Dutch oven coated with cooking spray over medium-high heat. Add chopped onion and celery; sauté 5 minutes or until tender. Add 1 teaspoon garlic, and sauté 1 minute. Add potato, ¼ teaspoon salt, and ¾ teaspoon pepper; cook 2 minutes. Lightly spoon flour into a dry measuring cup; level with a knife. Sprinkle flour over potato mixture, and cook 1 minute, stirring frequently. Add clam juice and milk; bring to a boil, stirring constantly. Cover, reduce heat, and simmer 20 minutes or until potato is tender. Partially mash potato using a potato masher. Stir in remaining ¼ teaspoon salt, remaining ¼ teaspoon pepper, Pernod, and thyme; simmer 10 minutes. Add scallops and half-and-half; cook 5 minutes or until scallops are done. Sprinkle with chives.

Calories 353; Fat 8.3g (sat 4.6g, mono 2.2g, poly 0.2g); Protein 33.8g; Carb 32.2g; Fiber 2.1g; Chol 99mg; Iron 3.4mg; Sodium 689mg; Calc 216mg

WINE TIP

With its splash of licorice-laced Pernod, this chowder is reminiscent of a bouillabaisse. And that makes the classic Provençal pairing, rosé wine, ideal. These fruity, affordable pink wines boast bright acidity and little tannin, which allows the subtle, sweet scallops to shine.

Simple Clam Chowder

This clam chowder recipe is easy and tastes even better the next day. Garnish with additional fresh thyme.

Yield: 12 servings (serving size: 1 cup soup)

2 bacon slices

2 cups chopped onion

1¼ cups chopped celery

½ teaspoon salt

½ teaspoon dried thyme

2 garlic cloves, minced

6 (6½-ounce) cans chopped clams, undrained

5 cups diced peeled baking potato (about 1 pound)

4 (8-ounce) bottles clam juice

1 bay leaf

2.25 ounces all-purpose flour (about ½ cup)

3 cups fat-free milk

1. Cook bacon in a large Dutch oven over medium heat until crisp. Remove bacon from pan, reserving 1 teaspoon bacon drippings in pan. Crumble bacon; set aside. Add onion, celery, salt, thyme, and garlic to drippings in pan; cook 4 minutes or until vegetables are tender.

2. Drain clams, reserving liquid. Add clam liquid, potato, clam juice, and bay leaf to pan; bring to a boil. Reduce heat, and simmer 15 minutes or until potato is tender. Discard bay leaf.

3. Lightly spoon flour into a dry measuring cup; level with a knife. Combine flour and milk, stirring with a whisk until smooth. Add flour mixture to pan; bring to a boil. Cook 12 minutes or until thick, stirring constantly. Add clams; cook 2 minutes. Sprinkle with reserved bacon.

Calories 257; Fat 2.9g (sat 0.6g, mono 0.6g, poly 0.7g); Protein 28.5g; Carb 27.9g; Fiber 2g; Chol 67mg; Iron 26.6mg; Sodium 475mg; Calc 242mg

Oyster and Wild Rice Bisque

Reminiscent of chowder, this bisque is a touch lighter, filled out with wild rice rather than the more common potatoes. Use salt pork—an old New England favorite—for bacon, if you prefer.

Yield: 8 servings (serving size: about ¾ cup soup)

1½ bacon slices, chopped

2 cups chopped onion (about 2 medium)

2 cups shucked oysters, undrained

1 cup clam juice

1 tablespoon all-purpose flour

1 cup fat-free, lower-sodium chicken broth

1 bay leaf

1½ cups cooked wild rice

1¼ cups whole milk

3 tablespoons half-and-half

½ teaspoon kosher salt

¼ teaspoon freshly ground black pepper

Chopped fresh flat-leaf parsley (optional)

1. Cook bacon in a large, heavy saucepan over medium-low heat 6 minutes or until crisp. Stir in onion; cover and cook 8 minutes or until onion is tender, stirring occasionally.

2. Strain oysters through a sieve over a bowl. Reserve oysters; add oyster liquid to pan. Combine clam juice and flour in a small bowl; stir with a whisk until smooth. Add clam juice mixture, broth, and bay leaf to pan. Increase heat to medium-high. Bring to a boil; cook until reduced to 2 cups (about 6 minutes).

3. Reduce heat to low. Discard bay leaf. Stir in rice, milk, half-and-half, salt, and pepper. Cover and simmer 10 minutes. Stir in reserved oysters; cook 5 minutes or until edges of oysters curl. Sprinkle with chopped fresh parsley, if desired.

Calories 141; Fat 5.2g (sat 2.1g, mono 1.4g, poly 0.8g); Protein 8.2g; Carb 15.5g; Fiber 1.3g; Chol 43mg; Iron 4.6mg; Sodium 357mg; Calc 91mg

Plum Island Sound Clam Chowder

If fresh clams are available, use about 1½ cups chopped clams. (Pictured on page 170.)

Yield: 10 servings (serving size: 1 cup soup)

4 (6½-ounce) cans chopped clams

2 (8-ounce) bottles clam juice

5 slices center-cut bacon, cut into ½-inch pieces

¾ cup chopped onion

½ cup chopped celery

1½ teaspoons butter

2 cups cubed red potato

1 tablespoon fresh thyme leaves

½ teaspoon salt

¼ teaspoon freshly ground black pepper

1 bay leaf

2¼ cups evaporated fat-free milk

1½ cups 1% low-fat milk

1½ tablespoons dry sherry

1 tablespoon chopped fresh parsley

1. Drain clams in a colander over a bowl, reserving juice. Add bottled clam juice to reserved juice to equal 3½ cups. Set aside clams and juice.
2. Cook bacon in a Dutch oven over medium heat until crisp, stirring occasionally. Remove bacon from pan with a slotted spoon, reserving 2 teaspoons bacon drippings in pan. Return bacon to pan; increase heat to medium-high. Add onion, celery, and butter; sauté 6 minutes or until vegetables are tender.
3. Add clam juice mixture, potato, and next 4 ingredients (through bay leaf); bring to a boil. Cover, reduce heat, and simmer 15 minutes or until potato is tender. Stir in clams, evaporated milk, 1% milk, and sherry. Cook 5 minutes or until thoroughly heated, stirring occasionally. Discard bay leaf. Sprinkle with parsley.

Calories 145; Fat 3.7g (sat 1.5g, mono 1.3g, poly 0.4g); Protein 12.1g; Carb 16.2g; Fiber 0.8g; Chol 23mg; Iron 5.6mg; Sodium 476mg; Calc 248mg

Quick Chicken-Corn Chowder

You can have this chicken corn chowder on the table in less than 30 minutes.

Yield: 6 servings (serving size: about 1 cup soup)

2 tablespoons butter

¼ cup chopped onion

¼ cup chopped celery

1 jalapeño pepper, seeded and minced

2 tablespoons all-purpose flour

3 cups 2% reduced-fat milk

2 cups chopped roasted skinless, boneless chicken breast (about 2 breast halves)

1½ cups fresh or frozen corn kernels (about 3 ears)

1 teaspoon chopped fresh or ¼ teaspoon dried thyme

¼ teaspoon ground red pepper

⅛ teaspoon salt

1 (14¾-ounce) can cream-style corn

1. Melt butter in a large Dutch oven over medium heat. Add onion, celery, and jalapeño; cook 3 minutes or until tender, stirring frequently. Add flour; cook 1 minute, stirring constantly. Stir in milk and remaining ingredients. Bring to a boil; cook until thick (about 5 minutes).

Calories 257; Fat 8.1g (sat 4.4g, mono 2.4g, poly 0.8g); Protein 19.1g; Carb 28.6g; Fiber 1.9g; Chol 52mg; Iron 0.4mg; Sodium 668mg; Calc 165mg

INGREDIENT TIP

May to September is the prime time for the two most common varieties of fresh corn: white corn, which has small, sweeter kernels; and yellow corn, with its large, full-flavored kernels. Choose ears with bright green, close-fitting husks, golden brown silk, and plump kernels in tightly spaced rows.

Chupe de Pollo con Chipotle *(Chicken Chowder with Chipotle)*

This hearty soup makes enough to feed a crowd and is simple to prepare on a weeknight.

Yield: 8 servings (serving size: about 1⅓ cups soup)

1 (7-ounce) can chipotle chiles in adobo sauce

1 tablespoon extra-virgin olive oil

2 cups chopped onion

1 cup chopped carrot

½ cup chopped celery

1 teaspoon ground cumin

½ teaspoon dried oregano

½ teaspoon dried thyme

6 garlic cloves, crushed

6 cups fat-free, lower-sodium chicken broth

1½ pounds skinless, boneless chicken breast

2 medium red potatoes (about 12 ounces), cut into ½-inch pieces

1 (15.5-ounce) can white or golden hominy, rinsed and drained

¼ cup whipping cream

1 cup chopped seeded plum tomato

¼ cup chopped fresh cilantro

½ teaspoon salt

8 lime wedges

1. Remove 1 chile and 1 teaspoon adobo sauce from can; reserve remaining chiles and sauce for another use. Finely chop chile; set chile and sauce aside separately. Heat oil in a large Dutch oven over medium heat. Add chopped chile, onion, and next 6 ingredients (through garlic); cook 7 minutes or until onion is tender, stirring frequently. Stir in broth; bring to a boil. Add chicken; cover, reduce heat to medium-low, and simmer 30 minutes or until chicken is tender. Remove chicken with a slotted spoon, and cool slightly. Shred chicken with 2 forks; cover and keep warm.

2. Remove pan from heat; let stand 5 minutes. Place one-third of broth mixture in a blender; process until smooth. Pour pureed broth mixture into a large bowl. Repeat procedure in two more batches with remaining broth mixture. Return pureed broth mixture to pan. Stir in potatoes and hominy; bring to a simmer over medium heat. Cook, uncovered, 20 minutes or until potatoes are tender. Stir in chicken and cream; simmer 5 minutes. Remove from heat, and stir in reserved adobo sauce, tomato, cilantro, and salt. Serve with lime wedges.

Calories 246; Fat 6.2g (sat 2.3g, mono 2.4g, poly 0.8g); Protein 24.5g; Carb 21.8g; Fiber 3.5g; Chol 60mg; Iron 1.7mg; Sodium 672mg; Calc 52mg

vegetable
soups

Apple-Parsnip Soup

Pink Lady apples are wonderful for applesauce, so they are ideal in this pureed appetizer soup. Sweet Fuji or all-purpose Spartan apples would also work well.

Yield: 8 servings (serving size: ¾ cup soup)

2 tablespoons olive oil

1 cup chopped onion

2½ cups chopped peeled Pink Lady apple (about 1 pound)

1 tablespoon curry powder

1½ teaspoons grated peeled fresh ginger

1 teaspoon ground cardamom

1 garlic clove, chopped

3½ cups chopped peeled parsnip (about 1½ pounds)

4 cups fat-free, lower-sodium chicken broth

1 cup apple cider

½ teaspoon salt

⅛ teaspoon freshly ground black pepper

8 teaspoons crème fraîche

Dash of freshly ground black pepper (optional)

1. Heat olive oil in a Dutch oven over medium heat. Add onion; cook 5 minutes or until tender, stirring frequently. Add apple and next 4 ingredients (through garlic); cook 1 minute, stirring constantly. Add parsnip, chicken broth, and apple cider; bring to a boil. Cover, reduce heat, and simmer 30 minutes or until parsnip is tender.

2. Place half of parsnip mixture in a blender. Remove center piece of blender lid (to allow steam to escape); secure blender lid on blender. Place a clean towel over opening in blender lid (to avoid splatters). Blend until smooth. Pour into a large bowl. Repeat procedure with remaining parsnip mixture. Stir in salt and pepper. Ladle about ¾ cup soup into each of 8 bowls; top each serving with 1 teaspoon crème fraîche. Garnish with a dash of black pepper, if desired.

Calories 136; Fat 5.6g (sat 1.6g, mono 2.6g, poly 0.6g); Protein 1.8g; Carb 21.2g; Fiber 4.2g; Chol 5mg; Iron 0.7mg; Sodium 381mg; Calc 30mg

Carrot-Parsnip Soup with Parsnip Chips

Winter root vegetables lend their complementary, slightly sweet flavors to this hearty bowl. Stir in more water or broth if you prefer a thinner consistency.

Yield: 6 servings (serving size: 1⅓ cups soup and about 2 teaspoons parsnip chips)

6 teaspoons olive oil, divided

2½ cups chopped yellow onion

3 cups coarsely chopped parsnip (about 1 pound)

3 cups water

2½ cups coarsely chopped carrot (about 1 pound)

2 (14-ounce) cans fat-free, lower-sodium chicken broth

¼ teaspoon salt

¼ teaspoon freshly ground black pepper

½ cup (⅛-inch-thick) slices parsnip

1 tablespoon chopped fresh chives

1. Heat 1 teaspoon oil in a Dutch oven over medium heat. Add onion, and cook 10 minutes or until tender, stirring occasionally. Add chopped parsnip, 3 cups water, carrot, and broth; bring to a boil. Reduce heat, and simmer 50 minutes or until vegetables are tender. Remove from heat; let stand 5 minutes.

2. Place half of carrot mixture in a blender. Remove center piece of blender lid (to allow steam to escape); secure blender lid on blender. Place a clean towel over opening in blender lid (to avoid splatters). Process until smooth. Pour pureed carrot mixture into a large bowl. Repeat procedure with remaining carrot mixture. Stir in salt and pepper.

3. Heat remaining 5 teaspoons oil in a small saucepan over medium-high heat. Add parsnip slices; cook 5 minutes or until lightly browned, turning occasionally. Drain on paper towels. Sprinkle parsnip chips and chives over soup.

Calories 159; Fat 4.9g (sat 0.7g, mono 3.4g, poly 0.6g); Protein 3.7g; Carb 26.4g; Fiber 6.4g; Chol 0mg; Iron 0.8mg; Sodium 388mg; Calc 61mg

Butternut Squash Soup with Spiced Seeds

You'll find pumpkinseed kernels—also called pepitas—at gourmet grocers and Mexican markets. We call for butternut squash in the recipe, but you can also use an heirloom variety of winter squash.

Yield: 8 servings (serving size: 1 cup soup)

1 tablespoon powdered sugar

1 tablespoon brown sugar

1 tablespoon egg white, lightly beaten

¼ teaspoon water

⅛ teaspoon salt

⅛ teaspoon ground cinnamon

Dash of ground red pepper

¾ cup unsalted pumpkinseed kernels

Cooking spray

1 (3½-pound) butternut squash

1 tablespoon canola oil

¼ teaspoon kosher salt, divided

4 cups fat-free, lower-sodium chicken broth

2 cups water

1. Preheat oven to 300°.

2. Combine first 7 ingredients in a small bowl. Add seeds to sugar mixture, stirring to coat. Spread seed mixture evenly on a baking sheet lined with parchment paper and coated with cooking spray. Bake at 300° for 15 minutes. Stir mixture; bake an additional 15 minutes. Place parchment on a wire rack; cool pumpkinseed mixture. Break into small pieces; set aside.

3. Increase oven temperature to 350°.

4. Cut squash in half lengthwise; discard seeds and membrane. Brush oil over cut sides of squash; sprinkle cut sides with ⅛ teaspoon salt. Place squash, cut sides down, on a jelly-roll pan. Bake at 350° for 1 hour and 20 minutes or until squash is tender. Cool slightly. Scoop out squash pulp from skins; discard skins.

5. Place squash pulp and broth in a blender. Remove center piece of blender lid (to allow steam to escape); secure blender lid on blender. Place a clean towel over opening in blender lid (to avoid splatters). Blend until smooth. Pour pureed mixture into a medium saucepan; stir in 2 cups water and remaining salt. Cook over medium-high heat 5 minutes or until thoroughly heated. Top each serving with spiced seeds.

Calories 130; Fat 3.2g (sat 0.4g, mono 1.5g, poly 1.1g); Protein 4.4g; Carb 24.1g; Fiber 5.1g; Chol 0mg; Iron 1.2mg; Sodium 395mg; Calc 76mg

Creamy Carrot and Sweet Potato Soup

You can make the soup several days in advance, and reheat it over medium-low heat. (Pictured on page 200.)

Yield: 8 servings (serving size: 1 cup soup)

3 tablespoons butter, divided

1 cup chopped onion

¼ teaspoon ground cinnamon

¼ teaspoon ground nutmeg

4¾ cups cubed peeled sweet potatoes (about 1½ pounds)

3½ cups water

3 cups fat-free, lower-sodium chicken broth

3 cups chopped carrot (about 1 pound)

¼ cup half-and-half

½ teaspoon salt

¼ teaspoon freshly ground black pepper

⅓ cup reduced-fat sour cream

2 tablespoons chopped fresh flat-leaf parsley

1. Melt 1 tablespoon butter in a large Dutch oven over medium heat. Add onion to pan; cook 4 minutes or until tender, stirring occasionally. Stir in cinnamon and nutmeg; cook 1 minute, stirring constantly. Move onion mixture to side of pan; add remaining 2 tablespoons butter to open space in pan. Increase heat to medium-high; cook 1 minute or until butter begins to brown. Add sweet potatoes, 3½ cups water, broth, and carrot; bring to a boil. Cover, reduce heat, and simmer 35 minutes or until vegetables are tender.
2. Place half of soup mixture in a blender. Remove center piece of blender lid (to allow steam to escape); secure blender lid on blender. Place a clean towel over opening in blender lid (to avoid splatters). Blend until smooth. Pour into a large bowl. Repeat procedure with remaining soup mixture. Stir in half-and-half, salt, and pepper. Ladle about 1 cup soup into each of 8 bowls; top each serving with about 2 teaspoons sour cream and ¾ teaspoon parsley.

Calories 173; Fat 6.7g (sat 4.1g, mono 1.5g, poly 0.3g); Protein 3.6g; Carb 25.7g; Fiber 5g; Chol 18mg; Iron 1mg; Sodium 415mg; Calc 77mg

INGREDIENT TIP

Look for sweet potatoes that are small to medium in size with few bruises and smooth skin. For optimal storage lasting three or four weeks, keep your sweet potatoes in a dark, dry, and cool (around 55 degrees) environment. They keep best when not stored in the refrigerator where they can develop a hard core.

White Velvet Soup

Celeriac and potatoes are the base of this deceptively rich soup. Serve it as the first course of a refined menu.

Yield: 6 servings (serving size: 1⅓ cups soup)

4 cups (¼-inch) diced peeled celeriac (celery root; about 1¼ pounds)

4 cups (¼-inch) diced peeled Yukon Gold potato (about 1¼ pounds)

3 cups fat-free, lower-sodium chicken broth

2 cups water

2 tablespoons fresh thyme leaves

4 large garlic cloves, chopped

⅓ cup white wine

½ cup 2% reduced-fat milk

1 tablespoon extra-virgin olive oil

3 tablespoons thinly sliced green onions

1. Combine first 6 ingredients in a large stockpot; bring to a boil. Partially cover, reduce heat, and simmer 30 minutes or until vegetables are tender. Place half of potato mixture in a blender. Remove center piece of blender lid (to allow steam to escape); secure blender lid on blender. Place a clean towel over opening in blender lid (to avoid splatters). Process until smooth. Pour pureed mixture into a large bowl. Repeat with remaining potato mixture. Return pureed potato mixture to pan; stir in wine. Cook over medium heat 3 minutes or until thoroughly heated. Remove soup from heat, and stir in milk.
2. Divide soup evenly among 6 bowls; drizzle oil evenly over soup. Sprinkle with onions.

Calories 167; Fat 3.1g (sat 0.7g, mono 2g, poly 0.4g); Protein 5.7g; Carb 28.0g; Fiber 4.1g; Chol 2mg; Iron 1.6mg; Sodium 398mg; Calc 88mg

Roasted Orange-and-Bell Pepper Soup

You can make the soup up to two days ahead, cover and chill it in the refrigerator. To serve, reheat it over low heat.

Yield: 2 servings (serving size: 1¼ cups soup)

1 large navel orange

1 large yellow bell pepper

2 teaspoons butter

½ cup chopped onion

⅓ cup grated carrot

1½ teaspoons all-purpose flour

1 cup fat-free, lower-sodium chicken broth

½ cup 1% low-fat milk

⅛ teaspoon black pepper

⅛ teaspoon paprika

Quartered orange slices (optional)

1. Cut orange in half crosswise; slice about ¼ inch from bottom of each half so they will sit flat. Cut bell pepper in half lengthwise; discard seeds and membranes. Place orange halves, cut sides up, and pepper halves, skin sides up, on a foil-lined baking sheet; flatten peppers with hand. Broil 15 minutes or until blackened.

2. Place pepper halves in a zip-top plastic bag; seal. Let stand 20 minutes; peel. Squeeze juice from orange over a bowl to equal ¼ cup; discard oranges. Place peppers and orange juice in a food processor or blender; set aside.

3. Heat butter in a small saucepan over medium heat. Add onion and carrot; sauté 12 minutes or until carrot is tender. Add onion mixture to food processor; process until smooth.

4. Combine flour, broth, and milk in saucepan; stir with a whisk until blended. Place over medium heat; bring to a boil. Reduce heat; add bell pepper mixture, black pepper, and paprika; simmer 10 minutes, stirring occasionally. Garnish with oranges, if desired.

Calories 144; Fat 4.9g (sat 2.9g, mono 1.2g, poly 0.3g); Protein 5.5g; Carb 21.0g; Fiber 3.9g; Chol 13mg; Iron 0.7mg; Sodium 356mg; Calc 117mg

Melanie's Garden-Tomato Soup

Delicious warm or chilled, this is a versatile soup that can be enjoyed on the hottest summer day or late in tomato season, when the weather is a bit cooler.

Yield: 5 servings (serving size: 1 cup soup)

2 teaspoons olive oil

¾ cup chopped onion

1 tablespoon chopped fresh oregano or basil

1 teaspoon chopped fresh or ¼ teaspoon dried thyme

2 garlic cloves, chopped

5 cups diced tomato (about 2 pounds)

1½ cups water

2½ tablespoons tomato paste

2 teaspoons sugar

¼ teaspoon salt

¼ teaspoon black pepper

Thinly sliced fresh basil (optional)

1. Heat olive oil in a large saucepan over medium heat. Add onion, oregano, thyme, and garlic; cook 4 minutes, stirring frequently. Stir in tomato and next 5 ingredients (through pepper). Bring to a boil. Reduce heat; simmer 15 minutes. Place half of soup in a blender or food processor. Remove center piece of blender lid (to allow steam to escape); secure blender lid on blender. Place a clean towel over opening in blender lid (to avoid splatters). Process until smooth, and pour into a bowl. Repeat procedure with remaining soup. Serve warm or chilled. Sprinkle with fresh basil, if desired.

Calories 81; Fat 2.6g (sat 0.4g, mono 1.4g, poly 0.5g); Protein 2.3g; Carb 14.6g; Fiber 2.9g; Chol 0mg; Iron 1.3mg; Sodium 140mg; Calc 29mg

Green Curry with Bok Choy

Yield: 4 servings (serving size: ½ cup rice and 1½ cups tofu mixture)

½ cup chopped fresh cilantro

2 tablespoons chopped peeled fresh ginger

2 teaspoons ground coriander

2 teaspoons ground cumin

8 garlic cloves, peeled

3 small serrano chiles, seeded

2 large shallots, coarsely chopped

4 cups coarsely chopped broccoli florets (about 1 head)

2 cups (½-inch-thick) slices baby bok choy

2 teaspoons dark sesame oil

4 teaspoons sugar

1 tablespoon lower-sodium soy sauce

¾ teaspoon kosher salt

3 Kaffir lime leaves

1 (13.5-ounce) can light coconut milk

1 (14-ounce) package water-packed organic firm tofu, drained and cut into ¾-inch cubes

¼ cup fresh lime juice

2 cups hot cooked long-grain white rice

¼ cup chopped fresh basil

2 tablespoons chopped fresh mint

1. Combine first 7 ingredients in a food processor; process until smooth. Set aside.

2. Cook broccoli florets in boiling water in a large Dutch oven 3 minutes or until crisp-tender. Remove broccoli from water with a slotted spoon; drain and rinse with cold water. Drain; set aside.

3. Return water to a boil. Add baby bok choy to pan; cook 1 minute. Drain and rinse with cold water. Drain; set aside.

4. Heat Dutch oven over medium-high heat. Add oil to pan; swirl to coat. Add cilantro mixture to pan; sauté 1 minute, stirring constantly. Add sugar and next 4 ingredients to pan; bring to a boil. Add tofu; cover, reduce heat, and simmer 6 minutes or until slightly thick. Add broccoli, bok choy, and juice; cook 1 minute or until heated, tossing to combine. Discard lime leaves.

5. Place ½ cup rice in each of 4 bowls; spoon 1½ cups tofu mixture over each serving. Sprinkle 1 tablespoon basil and 1½ teaspoons mint over each serving.

Calories 338; Fat 12.8g (sat 5.3g, mono 2.2g, poly 4.1g); Protein 16.6g; Carb 44.2g; Fiber 4.1g; Chol 0mg; Iron 5.0mg; Sodium 566mg; Calc 333mg

Chunky Tomato-Fruit Gazpacho

The mangoes, melons, and nectarines, along with the cucumber, give this gazpacho a sweet spin. Don't seed the jalapeño if you like a soup with more zip.

Yield: 7 servings (serving size: 1 cup soup)

2 cups finely chopped tomatoes (about ¾ pound)

2 cups finely diced honeydew melon (about ¾ pound)

2 cups finely diced cantaloupe (about ¾ pound)

1 cup finely diced mango (about 1 medium)

1 cup finely diced seeded peeled cucumber (about 1 medium)

1 cup finely diced nectarines (about 3 medium)

1 cup fresh orange juice (about 4 oranges)

½ cup finely chopped Vidalia or other sweet onion

¼ cup chopped fresh basil

3 tablespoons chopped fresh mint

3 tablespoons fresh lemon juice

1 teaspoon sugar

½ teaspoon salt

1 jalapeño pepper, seeded and finely chopped

1. Combine all ingredients in a large bowl. Cover and chill at least 2 hours.

Calories 95; Fat 0.5g (sat 0.1g, mono 0.1g, poly 0.2g); Protein 2.1g; Carb 23g; Fiber 2.8g; Chol 0mg; Iron 0.9mg; Sodium 189mg; Calc 33mg

Cucumber Soup

This fresh first-course soup features the addition of avocado, which adds a creamy texture as well as gorgeous color.

Yield: 6 servings (serving size: 1½ cups soup)

11 large cucumbers (about 8 pounds), divided

¼ cup honey, divided

¼ cup rice wine vinegar

1 ripe avocado, peeled and seeded

2 teaspoons chopped fresh dill

¼ teaspoon salt

¼ teaspoon freshly ground black pepper

Cracked black pepper (optional)

Dill sprigs (optional)

1. Cut 5 cucumbers into 3-inch chunks. Place half of cucumber chunks and 1 tablespoon honey in a blender or food processor; process until smooth. Pour pureed cucumber mixture through a cheesecloth-lined sieve into a bowl. Repeat procedure with remaining cucumber chunks and 1 tablespoon honey. Cover and chill at least 8 hours. Peel, seed, and thinly slice remaining 6 cucumbers; place slices in a bowl. Add vinegar and remaining 2 tablespoons honey; toss well to coat. Cover and chill 8 hours or overnight.

2. Working with pureed cucumber mixture in sieve over bowl, press mixture lightly with a wooden spoon or rubber spatula to squeeze out juice; reserve juice, and discard solids.

3. Place half of marinated cucumber slices, avocado, and 1¾ cups cucumber juice in a blender or food processor; process until smooth. Pour cucumber mixture into a bowl. Repeat procedure with remaining cucumber slices and 1¾ cups cucumber juice; reserve any remaining juice for another use. Stir in chopped dill, salt, and pepper. Place 1½ cups soup in each of 6 bowls. Garnish with cracked black pepper and dill sprigs, if desired.

Calories 167; Fat 6g (sat 0.9g, mono 3.2g, poly 0.7g); Protein 3.8g; Carb 27.3g; Fiber 5.3g; Chol 0mg; Iron 1.6mg; Sodium 312mg; Calc 79mg

WINE TIP

Green, vegetal flavors, like those found in this soup, call for sauvignon blanc's distinctive, herbaceous character. The wine's grassy, citrus qualities bring out the soup's crisp flavors.

Golden Gazpacho

Light and perfect for the summer, this recipe is a delicious and colorful way to use yellow heirloom tomatoes.

Yield: 6 servings (serving size: 1 cup soup)

3½ cups chopped seeded yellow tomato (about 1½ pounds)

2 cups chopped seeded peeled cucumber (about 1)

1 cup chopped yellow bell pepper (about 1 medium)

½ cup chopped red bell pepper

½ cup chopped green bell pepper

½ cup chopped red onion

2 garlic cloves, chopped

1 tablespoon chopped fresh mint

1 tablespoon chopped fresh cilantro

2 tablespoons white wine vinegar

1 tablespoon honey

2 teaspoons extra-virgin olive oil

¾ teaspoon salt

¼ teaspoon ground cumin

1. Combine the first 7 ingredients in a blender; process until smooth. Add mint and remaining ingredients; pulse 5 times or until well combined. Cover and chill at least 1 hour or overnight.

Calories 77; Fat 2.3g (sat 0.3g, mono 1.2g, poly 0.4g); Protein 2.9g; Carb 13.9g; Fiber 2.7g; Chol 0mg; Iron 1.4mg; Sodium 342mg; Calc 37mg

Roasted Tomato Tortilla Soup

Roasting tomatoes brings out their natural sweetness, so even if you don't have perfect summer tomatoes, you'll enjoy this soup.

Yield: 8 servings (serving size: 1 cup soup)

5 medium tomatoes, cut in half (about 1½ pounds)

2 (6-inch) Anaheim chiles

7 (¼-inch-thick) slices onion

2 large garlic cloves, halved

Cooking spray

8 (6-inch) white corn tortillas, cut into ½-inch strips

1 tablespoon chopped fresh cilantro

2 teaspoons ground cumin

½ teaspoon sugar

¼ teaspoon freshly ground black pepper

1 (32-ounce) carton fat-free, lower-sodium chicken broth

1 cup water

½ cup diced ripe avocado

½ cup (2 ounces) shredded queso fresco

8 cilantro sprigs

1. Preheat broiler.

2. Arrange tomatoes, cut sides down, on a foil-lined baking sheet. Cut chiles in half lengthwise; discard seeds and membranes. Place chiles, skin sides up, on baking sheet; flatten with hand. Broil 15 minutes or until blackened. Remove from oven; let stand 15 minutes. Peel tomatoes and chiles; place in a small bowl. Place onion and garlic on baking sheet; lightly coat with cooking spray. Broil 20 minutes or until browned, turning after 10 minutes. Add onion and garlic to tomatoes in bowl. Discard foil.

3. Arrange tortilla strips in a single layer on a baking sheet; coat with cooking spray. Broil 9 minutes or until lightly browned, stirring occasionally.

4. Place tomatoes, chiles, onion, and garlic in a food processor. Process 1 minute or until blended. Spoon tomato mixture into a large saucepan; cook over medium heat 2 minutes, stirring constantly. Reduce heat to low; cook 6 minutes, stirring occasionally. Stir in cilantro and next 5 ingredients (through water); bring to a boil. Cover, reduce heat, and simmer 15 minutes. Ladle 1 cup soup into each of 8 bowls; top each serving with about 6 tortilla strips, 1 tablespoon avocado, 1 tablespoon queso fresco, and 1 cilantro sprig.

Calories 124; Fat 4.2g (sat 0.8g, mono 1.9g, poly 0.7g); Protein 5.5g; Carb 19.2g; Fiber 4.0g; Chol 2mg; Iron 0.9mg; Sodium 351mg; Calc 55mg

Spicy Black-and-Red Bean Soup

To use a slow cooker, combine everything in the pot, and cook on HIGH for the first hour; then turn the temperature down to LOW, and cook 7 more hours.

Yield: 10 servings (serving size: 1 cup soup)

Cooking spray

1½ cups chopped onion

1¼ cups sliced carrot

2 garlic cloves, minced

3 cups fat-free, lower-sodium chicken broth

2 teaspoons sugar

1 (16-ounce) package frozen shoepeg white corn

1 (15-ounce) can red beans or kidney beans, drained

1 (15-ounce) can black beans, drained

1 (14.5-ounce) can Mexican-style stewed tomatoes with jalapeño peppers and spices, undrained

1 (14.5-ounce) can no-salt-added diced tomatoes, undrained

1 (4.5-ounce) can chopped green chiles

1. Place a large Dutch oven over medium-high heat. Coat Dutch oven with cooking spray. Add onion, carrot, and garlic; sauté 5 minutes. Stir in broth and remaining ingredients; bring to a boil. Cover, reduce heat, and simmer 2 hours.

Calories 152; Fat 0.8g (sat 0.1g, mono 0.1g, poly 0.3g); Protein 7.8g; Carb 30.8g; Fiber 4.2g; Chol 0mg; Iron 1.9mg; Sodium 374mg; Calc 52mg

NUTRITION TIP

If you have the time, try dried beans instead of canned; especially if you buy quality, artisanal dried beans, you'll be rewarded with more flavor. Dried beans offer the same fiber and protein as their canned counterparts, but with the advantage of allowing you to control the amount of salt.

Summer Corn and White Bean Soup

This quick, fiber-packed soup is a terrific way to use fresh corn. Add a slight kick with a sprinkle of Monterey Jack cheese with jalapeño peppers just before serving.

Yield: 6 servings (serving size: about 1½ cups soup)

1 tablespoon canola oil

1 cup sliced green onions

¾ cup chopped cooked ham (about 4 ounces)

3 cups fresh corn kernels (about 5 ears)

½ teaspoon salt

2 (15-ounce) cans navy beans, rinsed and drained

2 (14-ounce) cans fat-free, lower-sodium chicken broth

2 (4.5-ounce) cans chopped green chiles, undrained

1. Heat canola oil in a Dutch oven over medium heat. Add onions and ham, and cook 3 minutes, stirring frequently. Stir in corn and remaining ingredients. Bring to a boil; reduce heat, and simmer 5 minutes or until thoroughly heated.

Calories 278; Fat 5.3g (sat 1g, mono 2.5g, poly 1.4g); Protein 17g; Carb 42.8g; Fiber 10.1g; Chol 16mg; Iron 4.2mg; Sodium 593mg; Calc 150mg

Two-Bean Soup with Kale

This hearty bean soup warms up chilly nights. Use any type of canned beans you happen to have on hand, and add rotisserie chicken or Italian sausage for added protein, if you wish.

Yield: 6 servings (serving size: about 1¼ cups soup)

3 tablespoons olive oil

1 cup chopped onion

½ cup chopped carrot

½ cup chopped celery

½ teaspoon salt, divided

2 garlic cloves, minced

4 cups organic vegetable broth, divided

7 cups stemmed, chopped kale (about 1 bunch)

2 (15-ounce) cans no-salt-added cannellini beans, rinsed, drained, and divided

1 (15-ounce) can no-salt-added black beans, rinsed and drained

½ teaspoon freshly ground black pepper

1 tablespoon red wine vinegar

1 teaspoon chopped fresh rosemary

1. Heat a large Dutch oven over medium-high heat. Add oil to pan; swirl to coat. Add onion, carrot, and celery; sauté 6 minutes or until tender. Stir in ¼ teaspoon salt and garlic; cook 1 minute. Stir in 3 cups vegetable broth and kale. Bring to a boil; cover, reduce heat, and simmer 3 minutes or until kale is crisp-tender.

2. Place half of cannellini beans and remaining 1 cup vegetable broth in a blender or food processor; process until smooth. Add pureed bean mixture, remaining cannellini beans, black beans, and pepper to soup. Bring to a boil; reduce heat, and simmer 5 minutes. Stir in remaining ¼ teaspoon salt, vinegar, and rosemary.

Calories 250; Fat 10.4g (sat 1.4g, mono 5.5g, poly 2.2g); Protein 11.8g; Carb 30.5g; Fiber 9.2g; Chol 0mg; Iron 3.8mg; Sodium 593mg; Calc 189mg

White Bean and Sausage Ragout with Tomatoes, Kale, and Zucchini

Chock-full of vegetables, this one-pot ragout—a thick, well-seasoned stew—takes the chill out of a winter evening. If you've never had kale, you'll delight in its sweet, earthy flavor.

Yield: 4 servings (serving size: 1¾ cups soup)

1 tablespoon olive oil

½ cup chopped onion

2 (4-ounce) links chicken sausage, cut into (½-inch) slices

1 zucchini, quartered and cut into (½-inch) slices (about 2 cups)

3 garlic cloves, peeled and crushed

6 cups chopped trimmed kale (about ½ pound)

½ cup water

2 (16-ounce) cans no-salt-added cannellini beans or other white beans, rinsed and drained

1 (14.5-ounce) can diced tomatoes, undrained

¼ teaspoon salt

¼ teaspoon freshly ground black pepper

1. Heat oil in a large skillet over medium-high heat. Sauté onion and sausage 4 minutes or until sausage is browned. Add zucchini and garlic; cook 2 minutes. Add kale and remaining ingredients; bring to a boil. Cover, reduce heat, and simmer 10 minutes or until thoroughly heated. Serve immediately.

Calories 259; Fat 8.8g (sat 2.1g, mono 2.5g, poly 0.7g); Protein 17.5g; Carb 29.4g; Fiber 6.5g; Chol 61mg; Iron 4.6mg; Sodium 753mg; Calcium 252mg

White Bean-Rajas Soup

This 30-minute soup gets its name from the cooked peppers that are called *rajas* in Spanish.

Yield: 5 servings (serving size: 1½ cups soup)

Cooking spray

2 cups chopped white onion

2 cups chopped seeded poblano chile

1 cup chopped red bell pepper

4 garlic cloves, minced

2 cups fat-free, lower-sodium chicken broth

1½ cups water

2 (15-ounce) cans no-salt-added navy beans, rinsed and drained

¼ cup fresh lime juice

2 tablespoons ground cumin

1 cup (4 ounces) shredded queso Chihuahua or Monterey Jack cheese

2½ tablespoons reduced-fat sour cream

1. Heat a Dutch oven over medium-high heat. Coat Dutch oven with cooking spray. Add onion, chile, bell pepper, and garlic; sauté 5 minutes. Add broth and 1½ cups water; bring to a boil. Cover, reduce heat, and simmer 10 minutes. Remove from heat. Add beans, juice, and cumin. Cover and let stand 5 minutes. Ladle about 1½ cups soup into each of 5 bowls, and top each serving with about 3 tablespoons cheese and 1½ teaspoons sour cream.

Calories 210; Fat 9g (sat 5g, mono 2.3g, poly 0.3g); Protein 11.7g; Carb 22.1g; Fiber 6.3g; Chol 23mg; Iron 2.6mg; Sodium 298mg; Calc 259mg

INGREDIENT TIP

Queso Chihuahua is a semi-soft, pale yellow cheese that can develop a tangy flavor as it ages. Look for it in Mexican markets. If you can't find it, is it similar to Monterey Jack or a mild cheddar.

Tofu Vegetable Hot Pot

Tame this fiery soup by seeding the chile. If you love heat, try using two chiles.

Yield: 4 servings (serving size: 2 cups soup and ½ cup rice)

1 teaspoon vegetable oil

Cooking spray

1 cup thinly sliced shallots

1 tablespoon matchstick-cut peeled fresh ginger

1 teaspoon ground turmeric

1 serrano chile, thinly sliced

1 garlic clove, minced

1½ cups shredded green cabbage

1 cup sliced shiitake mushroom caps (about 3 ounces)

½ cup (¼-inch-thick) diagonally cut carrot

1 cup water

3 tablespoons lower-sodium soy sauce

¼ teaspoon sea salt

1 (14-ounce) can light coconut milk

1 pound water-packed firm tofu, drained and cut into 1-inch cubes

2 tomatoes, cut into 1-inch-thick wedges

½ cup torn fresh basil leaves

¼ cup (1-inch) sliced green onions

2 cups hot cooked jasmine rice

4 lime wedges

1. Heat oil in a large nonstick saucepan coated with cooking spray over medium-high heat. Add shallots; sauté 2 minutes. Reduce heat to medium. Add ginger, turmeric, chile, and garlic; cook 1 minute, stirring constantly. Add cabbage, mushroom, and carrot; cook 2 minutes, stirring occasionally.
2. Stir in 1 cup water, soy sauce, salt, and coconut milk; bring to a boil. Add tofu. Reduce heat; simmer 5 minutes. Add tomato; simmer 3 minutes. Stir in basil and onions. Serve over rice with lime wedges.

Calories 395; Fat 13.9g (sat 5.8g, mono 0.6g, poly 0.6g); Protein 21.5g; Carb 56.2g; Fiber 4.9g; Chol 0mg; Iron 5.6mg; Sodium 459mg; Calc 167mg

Vegetarian Harira

Several spices give this chickpea and lentil soup its rich flavor, so you won't miss the lamb, the traditional meat used in the Moroccan dish. Pair the soup with baked pita wedges. Freeze the leftover mushroom broth to use in place of water in homemade vegetable soups.

Yield: 2 servings (serving size: 1½ cups soup)

1 tablespoon canola oil

½ cup chopped onion

¼ cup chopped celery

1 cup warm water

Pinch of saffron threads

¼ teaspoon salt, divided

⅛ teaspoon minced peeled fresh ginger

⅛ teaspoon ground red pepper

⅛ teaspoon ground cinnamon

1 garlic clove, minced

1 cup organic mushroom broth

¾ cup chopped seeded plum tomato

¼ cup dried small red lentils

1 (15-ounce) can no-salt-added chickpeas (garbanzo beans), drained

1½ tablespoons chopped fresh cilantro

1½ tablespoons chopped fresh parsley

1. Heat oil in a large saucepan over medium heat. Add onion and celery to pan; sauté 4 minutes or until tender. Combine 1 cup warm water and saffron; let stand 2 minutes. Add ⅛ teaspoon salt, ginger, red pepper, cinnamon, and garlic to pan; cook 1 minute. Add saffron mixture, broth, tomato, lentils, and chickpeas; bring to a boil. Reduce heat, and simmer 20 minutes or until lentils are tender. Stir in cilantro, parsley, and remaining ⅛ teaspoon salt.

Calories 323; Fat 8.9g (sat 0.6g, mono 4.3g, poly 2.5g); Protein 14.8g; Carb 47.2g; Fiber 9.7g; Chol 0mg; Iron 3.8mg; Sodium 611mg; Calc 95mg

Red Lentil Mulligatawny with Apple-Celery Salsa

This creamy soup will thicken as it cools. Thin with hot water, a tablespoon at a time, to reach the desired consistency. Lentils provide fiber, folate, and protein, as well as iron. The fresh topping adds vitamin C, plus a dose of quercetin.

Yield: 4 servings (serving size: 1 cup soup)

Salsa:

⅔ cup finely chopped Granny Smith apple

¼ cup finely chopped celery

1 tablespoon chopped fresh cilantro

1 tablespoon fresh lime juice

Soup:

3½ cups fat-free, lower-sodium chicken broth

1 cup dried small red lentils

1 cup chopped onion

1½ cups light coconut milk

3 tablespoons tomato paste

1 teaspoon grated peeled fresh ginger

½ teaspoon ground cumin

⅛ teaspoon ground turmeric

1 teaspoon fresh lime juice

½ teaspoon salt

¼ teaspoon freshly ground black pepper

1. Combine first 4 ingredients; cover and chill.

2. Combine broth, lentils, and onion in a Dutch oven over medium-high heat; bring to a boil. Cover, reduce heat, and simmer 15 minutes or until lentils are tender. Pour half of lentil mixture into a blender; let stand 5 minutes. Remove center piece of blender lid (to allow steam to escape); secure blender lid on blender. Place a clean towel over opening in blender lid (to avoid splatters). Process until smooth. Pour pureed lentil mixture into a bowl. Pour remaining lentil mixture into blender; process until smooth. Add coconut milk, tomato paste, ginger, cumin, and turmeric; process until smooth. Return coconut milk mixture and remaining pureed lentil mixture to pan. Cover and simmer over medium heat 10 minutes. Remove from heat; stir in 1 teaspoon juice, salt, and pepper. Ladle about 1 cup soup into each of 4 bowls; top each serving with ¼ cup salsa.

Calories 280; Fat 5.9g (sat 4.4g, mono 0.1g, poly 0.1g); Protein 17.6g; Carb 42.4g; Fiber 9.6g; Chol 0mg; Iron 4.1mg; Sodium 677mg; Calc 50mg

INGREDIENT TIP

Tender, savory lentils are a great way to get the fiber and protein of beans. Because of their small size and thin skins, lentils require no soaking and cook quickly. Some varieties, like French green lentils, retain their shape better than others. Other lentils, such as red, are great for thickening soups.

Navy Bean Soup

Ham hocks create a rich stock, and their smoky flavor permeates the entire dish.

Yield: 6 servings (serving size: about 1⅔ cups soup)

2¼ cups dried navy beans (about 1 pound)

6 cups warm water

1 small yellow onion, peeled

3 whole cloves

⅔ cup chopped celery

3 thyme sprigs

3 parsley sprigs

3 smoked ham hocks (about 1⅓ pounds)

1 bay leaf

3 cups chopped kale

2 cups (½-inch) cubed peeled Yukon gold potato

1½ cups chopped Vidalia or other sweet onion

⅔ cup thinly sliced carrot

1 teaspoon salt

¾ teaspoon freshly ground black pepper

2 tablespoons chopped fresh parsley

1. Sort and wash beans; place in a large Dutch oven. Cover with water to 2 inches above beans; bring to a boil. Cook 2 minutes; remove from heat. Cover and let stand 1 hour. Drain beans; rinse and drain.

2. Return beans to pan; cover with 6 cups warm water. Stud whole onion with cloves; place in pan. Add celery, thyme, parsley sprigs, ham hocks, and bay leaf; bring to a boil. Cover, reduce heat, and simmer 45 minutes.

3. Discard onion, thyme, parsley sprigs, and bay leaf. Remove ham hocks from pan; cool slightly. Remove meat from bones; finely chop to yield ⅓ cup meat. Discard bones, skin, and fat. Add meat, kale, potato, chopped onion, carrot, salt, and pepper to pan; stir well. Cover and simmer 30 minutes or until beans and vegetables are tender. Stir in parsley.

Calories 396; Fat 5.5g (sat 1.8g, mono 1.8g, poly 1.1g); Protein 22.7g; Carb 67g; Fiber 21.7g; Chol 12mg; Iron 6.2mg; Sodium 455mg; Calc 194mg

breads
& salads

Baguette

Try your hand at making this classic French bread—you'll love the result.

Yield: 2 loaves, 12 servings per loaf (serving size: 1 slice)

1 package dry yeast (about 2¼ teaspoons)

1¼ cups warm water (100° to 110°)

14.25 ounces bread flour, divided (about 3 cups)

1 teaspoon salt

Cooking spray

1 teaspoon cornmeal

1. Dissolve yeast in warm water in a large bowl; let stand 5 minutes. Lightly spoon flour into dry measuring cups; level with a knife. Add 2¾ cups flour to yeast mixture; stir until a soft dough forms. Cover and let stand 15 minutes. Turn dough out onto a lightly floured surface; sprinkle evenly with salt. Knead until salt is incorporated and dough is smooth and elastic (about 6 minutes); add enough of remaining flour, 1 tablespoon at a time, to prevent dough from sticking to hands (dough will feel slightly sticky).

2. Place dough in large bowl coated with cooking spray, turning to coat top. Cover and let rise in a warm place (85°), free from drafts, 40 minutes or until doubled in size. (Gently press two fingers into dough. If an indentation remains, dough has risen enough.) Punch dough down; cover and let rest 5 minutes. Divide in half. Working with one portion at a time (cover remaining dough to prevent drying), roll each portion on a floured surface into a 12-inch rope, slightly tapered at ends. Place ropes on a large baking sheet sprinkled with cornmeal. Lightly coat dough with cooking spray, and cover; let rise 20 minutes or until doubled in size.

3. Preheat oven to 450°.

4. Uncover dough. Cut 3 (¼-inch-deep) diagonal slits across top of each loaf. Bake at 450° for 20 minutes or until browned on bottom and sounds hollow when tapped.

Calories 53; Fat 0.2g (sat 0g, mono 0.1g, poly 0.1g); Protein 2.1g; Carb 11.2g; Fiber 0.5g; Chol 0mg; Iron 0.8mg; Sodium 97mg; Calc 1mg

Rosemary Focaccia

The rosemary steeps in boiling water; be sure to let it cool to within 100° to 110° before adding the yeast so your dough will rise correctly. Sea salt and kosher salt have larger crystals than regular salt, so either adds a nice crunch to the top of the bread. But be sure to use regular salt in the dough for best results. You don't need to use all the egg and oil mixture on top of the dough; spread enough to coat the top, and discard any extra.

Yield: 1 loaf, 14 servings per loaf (serving size: 1 slice)

1¼ cups boiling water

3 tablespoons chopped fresh rosemary, divided

1 tablespoon honey

1 package dry yeast (about 2¼ teaspoons)

16.9 ounces all purpose flour, divided (about 3¾ cups)

¼ cup olive oil, divided

1 teaspoon salt

Cooking spray

1 teaspoon water

1 large egg yolk

½ teaspoon sea salt or kosher salt

1. Combine boiling water, 1 teaspoon rosemary, and honey in a large bowl; cool to within 100° to 110°. Sprinkle yeast over honey mixture; let stand 5 minutes. Lightly spoon flour into dry measuring cups; level with a knife. Add 3¼ cups flour, 2 tablespoons oil, and 1 teaspoon salt to honey mixture, stirring to form a soft dough. Turn dough out onto a floured surface. Knead until smooth and elastic (about 10 minutes); add enough of remaining flour, 1 tablespoon at a time, to prevent dough from sticking to hands (dough will feel sticky).

2. Place dough in a large bowl coated with cooking spray, turning to coat top. Cover and let rise in a warm place (85°), free from drafts, 45 minutes or until doubled in size. (Gently press two fingers into dough. If indentation remains, dough has risen enough.) Punch dough down. Pat dough into a 14 x 12-inch rectangle on a baking sheet coated with cooking spray. Cover and let rise 20 minutes or until doubled in size.

3. Preheat oven to 350°.

4. Uncover dough. Make indentations in top of dough using handle of a wooden spoon or your fingertips. Combine 1 tablespoon oil, 1 teaspoon water, and egg yolk; brush over dough. Drizzle with remaining 1 tablespoon oil; sprinkle with remaining rosemary and sea salt.

5. Bake at 350° for 25 minutes or until lightly browned. Remove from pan; cool on a wire rack.

Calories 167; Fat 4.6g (sat 0.7g, mono 3g, poly 0.6g); Protein 3.9g; Carb 27.1g; Fiber 1.1g; Chol 15mg; Iron 1.8mg; Sodium 239mg; Calc 9mg

Fresh Whole-Wheat Pitas

These are sublime straight out of the oven and stuffed with your favorite salad or sandwich fixings. Leftovers make tasty chips. White whole-wheat flour is available through King Arthur (www.kingarthurflour.com) or Bob's Red Mill (www.bobsredmill.com).

Yield: 8 servings (serving size: 1 pita)

1 tablespoon sugar

1 package dry yeast (about 2¼ teaspoons)

1 cup plus 2 tablespoons warm water (100° to 110°)

10 ounces bread flour (about 2¼ cups)

4.75 ounces white whole-wheat flour (about 1 cup), divided

2 tablespoons 2% Greek-style yogurt

1 tablespoon extra-virgin olive oil

¾ teaspoon salt

Olive oil–flavored cooking spray

1. Dissolve sugar and yeast in 1 cup plus 2 tablespoons warm water in a large bowl; let stand 5 minutes. Lightly spoon flours into dry measuring cups; level with a knife. Add bread flour, 3 ounces (about ¾ cup) whole-wheat flour, yogurt, oil, and salt to the yeast mixture; beat with a mixer at medium speed until smooth. Turn dough out onto a floured surface. Knead dough until smooth and elastic (about 10 minutes); add enough of remaining whole-wheat flour, 1 tablespoon at a time, to prevent dough from sticking to hands (dough will feel sticky). Place dough in a large bowl coated with cooking spray, turning to coat top. Cover and let rise in a warm place (85°), free from drafts, 45 minutes or until doubled in size.

2. Position oven rack on lowest shelf.

3. Preheat oven to 500°.

4. Divide dough into 8 portions. Working with one portion at a time, gently roll each portion into a 5½-inch circle. Place 4 dough circles on each of 2 baking sheets heavily coated with cooking spray. Bake, 1 sheet at a time, at 500° for 8 minutes or until puffed and browned. Cool on a wire rack.

Calories 211; Fat 2.9g (sat 0.4g, mono 1.5g, poly 0.4g); Protein 7g; Carb 39.9g; Fiber 3.1g; Chol 0mg; Iron 2.5mg; Sodium 225mg; Calc 11mg

NUTRITION TIP

White whole-wheat flour is simply made from white wheat instead of the more traditional red wheat. White wheat doesn't have the genes for bran color, and it also has a milder flavor than red wheat. Nutritionally, though, it's considered equal to red wheat.

Buttered Sweet Potato Knot Rolls

Serve these beautifully-colored rolls for a holiday dinner. If you have leftover baked, mashed sweet potatoes, you can substitute them for the canned sweet potatoes called for in this recipe.

Yield: 24 servings (serving size: 1 roll)

1 package dry yeast (about 2¼ teaspoons)

1 cup warm 2% reduced-fat milk (100° to 110°)

¾ cup canned mashed sweet potatoes

3 tablespoons butter, melted and divided

1¼ teaspoons salt

2 large egg yolks, lightly beaten

23.75 ounces bread flour, divided (about 5 cups)

Cooking spray

1. Dissolve yeast in warm milk in a large bowl; let stand 5 minutes.

2. Add sweet potatoes, 1 tablespoon butter, salt, and egg yolks, stirring mixture with a whisk.

3. Lightly spoon flour into dry measuring cups; level with a knife. Add 4½ cups flour; stir until a soft dough forms.

4. Turn dough out onto a floured surface. Knead until smooth and elastic (about 8 minutes); add enough of remaining flour, 1 tablespoon at a time, to prevent dough from sticking to hands (dough will feel very soft and tacky).

5. Place dough in a large bowl coated with cooking spray, turning to coat top. Cover and let rise in a warm place (85°), free from drafts, 45 minutes or until doubled in size. (Gently press two fingers into dough. If indentation remains, dough has risen enough.) Punch dough down. Cover and let rest 5 minutes.

6. Line 2 baking sheets with parchment paper. Divide dough into 24 equal portions. Working with one portion at a time (cover remaining dough to prevent drying), shape each portion into a 9-inch rope. Carefully shape rope into a knot; tuck top end of knot under roll. Place roll on a prepared pan.

7. Repeat procedure with remaining dough, placing 12 rolls on each pan. Lightly coat rolls with cooking spray; cover and let rise 30 minutes or until doubled in size.

8. Preheat oven to 400°.

9. Uncover rolls. Bake at 400° for 8 minutes with 1 pan on bottom rack and 1 pan on second rack from top. Rotate pans; bake an additional 7 minutes or until rolls are golden brown on top and sound hollow when tapped.

10. Remove rolls from pans; place on wire racks. Brush rolls with remaining 2 tablespoons butter. Serve warm or at room temperature.

Calories 134; Fat 2.6g (sat 1.2g, mono 0.7g, poly 0.3g); Protein 4.3g; Carb 23g; Fiber 0.9g; Chol 22mg; Iron 1.4mg; Sodium 147mg; Calc 21mg

Flaky Dinner Rolls

These superlative rolls derive their texture and beautiful shape from employing a simple folding technique twice and allowing them to rise just once.

Yield: 12 servings (serving size: 1 roll)

3 tablespoons sugar

1 package dry yeast (about 2¼ teaspoons)

1 cup warm fat-free milk (100° to 110°)

13.5 ounces all-purpose flour (about 3 cups), divided

¾ teaspoon salt

3 tablespoons butter, softened

Cooking spray

1. Dissolve sugar and yeast in warm milk in a large bowl; let stand 5 minutes. Lightly spoon flour into dry measuring cups; level with a knife. Add 2¾ cups flour and salt to yeast mixture; stir until a dough forms. Turn dough out onto a lightly floured surface. Knead until smooth (about 5 minutes); add enough of remaining flour, 1 tablespoon at a time, to prevent dough from sticking to hands (dough will feel slightly sticky). Cover dough with plastic wrap, and let rest 10 minutes.

2. Roll dough into a 12 x 10-inch rectangle on a lightly floured baking sheet. Gently spread butter over dough. Working with a long side, fold up bottom third of dough. Fold top third of dough over the first fold to form a 12 x 3-inch rectangle. Cover with plastic wrap; place in freezer on baking sheet 10 minutes.

3. Remove dough from freezer; remove plastic wrap. Roll dough, still on baking sheet (sprinkle on a little more flour, if needed), into a 12 x 10-inch rectangle. Working with a long side, fold up bottom third of dough. Fold top third of dough over the first fold to form a 12 x 3-inch rectangle. Cover with plastic wrap; place in freezer on baking sheet 10 minutes.

4. Remove dough from freezer; remove plastic wrap. Roll dough, still on baking sheet, into a 12 x 8-inch rectangle. Beginning with a long side, roll up dough jelly-roll fashion; pinch seam to seal (do not seal ends of roll). Cut roll into 12 equal slices. Place slices, cut sides up, in muffin cups coated with cooking spray. Lightly coat tops of dough slices with cooking spray. Cover and let rise in a warm place (85°), free from drafts, 45 minutes or until doubled in size.

5. Preheat oven to 375°.

6. Bake at 375° for 20 minutes or until golden brown. Remove from pan, and cool 5 minutes on a wire rack. Serve rolls warm.

Calories 160; Fat 3.2g (sat 1.5g, mono 1.2g, poly 0.2g); Protein 4.2g; Carb 28.3g; Fiber 1g; Chol 8mg; Iron 1.7mg; Sodium 178mg; Calc 25mg

Parmesan-Corn Bread Muffins

The flavorful cheese in this recipe is a nice balance with the sweetness of cornmeal.

Yield: 10 servings (serving size: 1 muffin)

4.5 ounces all-purpose flour (about 1 cup)

⅔ cup yellow cornmeal

2 tablespoons sugar

2 teaspoons baking powder

¼ teaspoon salt

⅔ cup nonfat buttermilk

3 tablespoons vegetable oil

2 large egg whites, lightly beaten

Cooking spray

¼ cup (1 ounce) grated fresh Parmesan cheese

1. Preheat oven to 425°.

2. Lightly spoon flour and cornmeal into dry measuring cups; level with a knife. Combine flour, cornmeal, sugar, baking powder, and salt in a medium bowl, stirring with a whisk. Make a well in center of mixture. Combine buttermilk, oil, and egg whites; add to flour mixture, stirring just until moist.

3. Spoon batter into 10 muffin cups coated with cooking spray. Sprinkle evenly with cheese. Bake at 425° for 10 minutes or until muffins spring back when touched lightly in center. Remove muffins from pan immediately; place on a wire rack. Serve warm.

Calories 151; Fat 4.9g (sat 1.1g mono 1.2g poly 2.4g); Protein 4.3g; Carb 21.9g; Fiber 0.6g; Chol 2mg; Iron 1mg; Sodium 229mg; Calc 110mg

Whole Grain Cornsticks

You can prepare these in muffin tins, but a cast-iron cornstick pan yields a crisper crust.

Yield: 1 dozen (serving size: 1 cornstick)

3.6 ounces whole-wheat flour (about ¾ cup)

¾ cup yellow cornmeal

3 tablespoons grated fresh Parmesan cheese

2 teaspoons baking powder

1½ teaspoons chili powder

1 teaspoon salt

¾ cup plus 2 tablespoons fat-free milk

2 tablespoons olive oil

2 tablespoons honey

1 large egg, lightly beaten

¾ cup frozen whole-kernel corn, thawed

⅓ cup minced red onion

2 tablespoons minced jalapeño pepper

Cooking spray

1. Preheat oven to 425°.

2. Lightly spoon flour into a dry measuring cup; level with a knife. Combine flour and next 5 ingredients (through salt) in a large bowl. Make a well in center of mixture. Combine milk, oil, honey, and egg. Add to flour mixture, stirring just until moist. Fold in corn, onion, and jalapeño.

3. Place a cast-iron cornstick pan in 425° oven for 5 minutes. Remove from oven; immediately coat with cooking spray. Spoon batter into pan. Bake at 425° for 18 minutes or until lightly browned. Remove from pan immediately; serve warm.

Calories 120; Fat 3.6g (sat 0.8g, mono 2.1g, poly 0.4g); Protein 4g; Carb 19g; Fiber 2g; Chol 19mg; Iron 0.7mg; Sodium 325mg; Calc 96mg

Corn Bread Bites

This recipe also makes a dozen muffins in a standard muffin tin; bake for 17 minutes or until golden brown.

Yield: 12 servings (serving size: 3 muffins)

3 ounces all-purpose flour (about ⅔ cup)

½ cup yellow cornmeal

1 tablespoon sugar

1½ teaspoons baking powder

¼ teaspoon salt

½ cup (2 ounces) shredded sharp cheddar cheese

½ cup reduced-fat sour cream

¼ cup thinly sliced green onions

1 (8¾-ounce) can cream-style corn

Dash of hot sauce

1 large egg, lightly beaten

Cooking spray

1. Preheat oven to 375°.

2. Lightly spoon flour into dry measuring cup; level with a knife. Combine flour and next 4 ingredients (through salt) in a large bowl. Combine cheese and remaining ingredients except cooking spray in a small bowl; stir with a whisk. Add to flour mixture; stir just until moistened.

3. Divide batter evenly among miniature muffin cups coated with cooking spray. Bake at 375° for 10 minutes or until golden brown. Cool in cups 2 minutes on wire racks; remove from pans. Cool completely on wire racks.

Calories 108; Fat 3.4g (sat 1.9g, mono 0.5g, poly 0.1g); Protein 3.7g; Carb 15.5g; Fiber 0.8g; Chol 28mg; Iron 0.8mg; Sodium 221mg; Calc 89mg

MAKE AHEAD TIP

You also can double the recipe and freeze the extra muffins for up to one month. If you do this, prepare the muffins in two batches so the baking powder doesn't lose its effectiveness while the extra batter waits for the first batch to be turned out of the pans.

Crisp Croutons

Use these croutons on Pesto Caesar Salad (page 265) or to add crunch to any soup or salad.

Yield: 6 cups (serving size: 2 tablespoons croutons)

6 cups (½-inch) cubed sourdough or French bread (6 ounces)

1 tablespoon butter, melted

1 teaspoon paprika

1 teaspoon onion powder

1. Preheat oven to 350°.

2. Combine all ingredients in a roasting or jelly-roll pan; toss well to coat. Bake at 350° for 20 minutes or until toasted, turning once.

Calories 24; Fat 0.7g (sat 0.4g, mono 0.2g, poly 0.1g); Protein 0.7g; Carb 4g; Fiber 0.2g; Chol 1mg; Iron 0.2mg; Sodium 48mg; Calc 6mg

Spinach Strawberry Salad

This simple starter salad is an ideal accompaniment to grilled or roast chicken or pork.

Yield: 4 servings (serving size: 2 cups salad)

1½ cups quartered strawberries

¼ cup **Easy Herb Vinaigrette**

1 tablespoon finely chopped fresh mint

1 (6-ounce) package fresh baby spinach

2 tablespoons sliced almonds, toasted

¼ teaspoon freshly ground black pepper

1. Combine first 4 ingredients in a large bowl; toss gently to coat. Sprinkle with almonds and pepper; serve immediately.

Calories 136; Fat 10.3g (sat 0.7g, mono 6g, poly 3g); Protein 2.1g; Carb 11g; Fiber 3.6g; Chol 0mg; Iron 1.7mg; Sodium 113mg; Calc 50mg

Easy Herb Vinaigrette

Since this recipe makes plenty of dressing to keep on hand, having a salad with dinner is effortless any night of the week.

Yield: About 1⅔ cups (serving size: 2 tablespoons vinaigrette)

9 tablespoons white wine vinegar

1½ tablespoons wildflower honey

½ teaspoon fine salt

1 cup canola oil

3 tablespoons chopped fresh basil

3 tablespoons minced fresh chives

1. Combine first 3 ingredients in a medium bowl; slowly whisk in oil until combined. Stir in basil and chives. Store, covered, in refrigerator for up to 5 days.

Calories 160; Fat 17.2g (sat 1.2g, mono 10.2g, poly 5.1g); Protein 0.1g; Carb 2.1g; Fiber 0.1g; Chol 0mg; Iron 0mg; Sodium 89mg; Calc 2mg

Pike Place Market Salad

This salad calls for herb salad mix, which can be found prebagged in the supermarket, or you can use any combination of lettuces and herbs. Any fresh cherry or berry (such as blackberries or blueberries) will do nicely. The dressing and caramelized walnuts can be made a day ahead—store the nuts in an airtight container and the dressing in the refrigerator.

Yield: 4 servings (serving size: 2 cups salad)

Walnuts:

1 tablespoon sugar

3 tablespoons coarsely chopped walnuts

Cooking spray

Dressing:

½ cup apple cider

3 tablespoons water

¼ teaspoon cornstarch

1 tablespoon finely chopped shallots

1 tablespoon champagne vinegar

⅛ teaspoon salt

⅛ teaspoon freshly ground black pepper

Remaining ingredients:

8 cups herb salad mix

2 cups berries and/or pitted sweet cherries

¼ cup (1 ounce) blue cheese, crumbled

1. Place sugar in a small skillet over medium heat; cook 90 seconds or until sugar dissolves, stirring as needed so sugar dissolves evenly and doesn't burn. Reduce heat; stir in walnuts. Cook over low heat 30 seconds or until golden. Spread mixture onto foil coated with cooking spray. Cool completely; break into small pieces.

2. Place cider in a small saucepan over medium-high heat; bring to a boil. Cook until reduced to 2 tablespoons (about 5 minutes). Combine water and cornstarch in a small bowl; add to pan. Bring cider mixture to a boil, stirring constantly; cook 30 seconds. Remove from heat. Stir in shallots, vinegar, salt, and pepper; let cool.

3. Place salad mix in a large bowl. Drizzle with dressing; toss gently to coat. Divide evenly among 4 plates; top with berries, cheese, and walnuts. Serve immediately.

Calories 165; Fat 6.7g (sat 1.8g, mono 0.7g, poly 3g); Protein 5.2g; Carb 24.6g; Fiber 4.5g; Chol 6mg; Iron 1.9mg; Sodium 199mg; Calc 116mg

WINE NOTE

This market salad is a kaleidoscope of bold flavors and compelling textures, from the berries to the caramelized walnuts to the crumbled blue cheese. It needs a powerhouse of a wine to match it all; try a Gewürztraminer with bright tropical fruit flavors. It is a great counterpoint to the saltiness of the cheese.

Frisée Salad with Maple-Bacon Vinaigrette

Bitter greens like radicchio and endive provide a pleasant counterpoint to the sweet, slightly smoky dressing, while wispy, curly frisée gives the salad body. You can prepare the salad dressing up to a day ahead and reheat it to serve. Dress the salad at the last minute so the greens stay crisp.

Yield: 8 servings (serving size: about ¾ cup salad)

6 cups torn frisée leaves

4 cups (¾-inch) diagonally cut Belgian endive (about 3 heads)

1 cup thinly sliced radicchio

4 center-cut bacon slices

¼ cup chopped shallots

2 tablespoons champagne vinegar

4 teaspoons maple syrup

1 teaspoon extra-virgin olive oil

1 teaspoon Dijon mustard

¼ teaspoon salt

⅛ teaspoon freshly ground black pepper

3 ounces (about ¾ cup) crumbled blue cheese

1. Combine first 3 ingredients in a large bowl. Cook bacon in a large nonstick skillet over medium heat until crisp. Remove bacon from pan, reserving drippings; crumble. Add shallots to drippings in pan; cook 30 seconds, stirring constantly. Remove from heat; stir in champagne vinegar, maple syrup, extra-virgin olive oil, Dijon mustard, salt, and freshly ground black pepper. Pour dressing over salad greens; toss well to combine. Add crumbled bacon and cheese to greens; toss gently.

Calories 96; Fat 6g (sat 3g, mono 2.3g, poly 0.3g); Protein 5g; Carb 6.3g; Fiber 2g; Chol 13mg; Iron 0.7mg; Sodium 352mg; Calcium 94mg

Pesto Caesar Salad

Pesto pumps up the flavor in this version of a classic while getting rid of the calories and fat associated with the traditional Caesar salad. Instead of an egg-based dressing, the dressing is flavored with pesto.

Yield: 6 servings (serving size: 1⅓ cups salad)

3 ounces French bread baguette, cut into ½-inch cubes

1½ teaspoons extra-virgin olive oil

Cooking spray

2 ounces Parmigiano-Reggiano cheese

¼ cup organic canola mayonnaise

3 tablespoons refrigerated pesto

4 teaspoons water

2 teaspoons fresh lemon juice

1 teaspoon anchovy paste

½ teaspoon Worcestershire sauce

½ teaspoon Dijon mustard

⅛ teaspoon hot pepper sauce

1 garlic clove, minced

12 cups torn romaine lettuce

1. Preheat oven to 400°.

2. Place bread in a large bowl; drizzle with oil. Toss to coat. Arrange bread in a single layer on a baking sheet coated with cooking spray. Bake at 400° for 10 minutes or until golden, turning once.

3. Grate 2 tablespoons cheese; shave remaining cheese to equal about 6 tablespoons. Set shaved cheese aside.

4. Combine grated cheese, mayonnaise, and next 8 ingredients (through garlic) in a medium bowl, stirring well with a whisk. Combine croutons and lettuce in a large bowl. Drizzle mayonnaise mixture over lettuce mixture; toss to coat.

5. Place 1⅓ cups salad on each of 6 plates, and top each serving with 1 tablespoon shaved cheese.

Calories 202; Fat 14.3g (sat 2.3g, mono 6.2g, poly 5.4g); Protein 6.2g; Carb 13.6g; Fiber 2.9g; Chol 15mg; Iron 1.9mg; Sodium 331mg; Calc 131mg

INGREDIENT TIP

Parmigiano-Reggiano is one of the crucial flavors of a good Caesar salad— so treat yourself to the real thing. Only cheese that is produced in a limited area surrounding Parma, Italy, according to strict guidelines may be sold as Parmigiano-Reggiano. It's a cheese of incomparable flavor, texture, and richness that make it not only an excellent grating cheese, but also one of the world's great table cheeses.

Mixed Lettuce, Pear, and Goat Cheese Salad with Citrus Dressing

If you can't find Meyer lemons, use regular lemon juice and add a pinch of sugar to approximate the flavor.

Yield: 8 servings (serving size: about 1 cup lettuce mixture, about ¼ cup pear, and 1½ tablespoons cheese)

Dressing:

1 tablespoon finely chopped shallots

1 teaspoon Dijon mustard

¼ cup fresh orange juice

4 teaspoons fresh Meyer lemon juice

¼ teaspoon kosher salt

⅛ teaspoon freshly ground black pepper

4 teaspoons extra-virgin olive oil

Salad:

2 tablespoons fresh orange juice

2 firm ripe Bosc pears, cored and thinly sliced

6 cups mixed baby lettuces

1 head Boston or butter lettuce, torn (about 2 cups)

¾ cup (3 ounces) crumbled goat cheese

1. Combine shallots and mustard in a medium bowl, stirring with a whisk. Stir in ¼ cup orange juice and next 3 ingredients (through pepper). Gradually add oil, stirring constantly with a whisk.

2. Combine 2 tablespoons orange juice and pears, tossing to coat. Combine lettuces in a large bowl. Drizzle with dressing; toss gently to coat. Arrange about 1 cup lettuce mixture on each of 8 salad plates. Top each serving with about ¼ cup pear and 1½ tablespoons cheese.

Calories 100; Fat 5.6g (sat 2.5g, mono 2.4g, poly 0.4g); Protein 3.5g; Carb 10.2g; Fiber 2.5g; Chol 8mg; Iron 1.1mg; Sodium 141mg; Calc 67mg

Mixed Citrus Green Salad

The dressing on this salad also works well on fruit salads without greens, too.

Yield: 7 servings (serving size: 2 cups salad, 1 tablespoon dressing, and 3 walnut halves)

1 cup red seedless grapes, halved

2 (5-ounce) bags mixed salad greens

1 (11-ounce) can mandarin oranges, drained

1 (8-ounce) container pineapple chunks, drained

1 (8-ounce) container red grapefruit, drained

7 tablespoons Orange-Poppy Seed Dressing

21 walnut halves, toasted

1. Combine first 5 ingredients in a large bowl. Arrange 2 cups salad on each of 7 plates; drizzle with 1 tablespoon Orange-Poppy Seed Dressing (reserve remaining dressing for another use). Top each serving with 3 walnut halves.

Calories 173; Fat 8.6g (sat 1.4g, mono 2.3g, poly 3.8g); Protein 3.3g; Carb 23.5g; Fiber 2.3g; Chol 4mg; Iron 0.8mg; Sodium 53mg; Calc 60mg

Orange-Poppy Seed Dressing

Yield: 1 cup plus 2 tablespoons (serving size: 1 tablespoon dressing)

½ cup fresh orange juice

¼ cup honey

¼ cup canola oil

2 tablespoons champagne vinegar

⅛ teaspoon salt

1 teaspoon poppy seeds

1. Place first 5 ingredients in a blender; process until blended. Add poppy seeds; pulse once. Cover and refrigerate.

Calories 17; Fat 1.2g (sat 0.1g, mono 0.7g, poly 0.4g); Protein 0g; Carb 1.7g; Fiber 0g; Chol 0mg; Iron 0mg; Sodium 7mg; Calc 1mg

Arugula, Roasted Tomato, and Goat Cheese Salad

Use your favorite salad greens for this tasty first course. We liked the spiciness of arugula, but any other greens will work.

Yield: 6 servings (serving size: about 1⅓ cups salad and 1 teaspoon cheese)

1 cup grape or cherry tomatoes, halved

¼ cup Maple-Balsamic Dressing, divided

Cooking spray

8 cups loosely packed baby arugula, watercress, or spinach (about 4 ounces)

¼ cup thinly vertically sliced red onion

2 tablespoons crumbled goat cheese

¼ teaspoon freshly ground black pepper

1. Preheat oven to 350°.

2. Combine tomatoes and 2 tablespoons Maple-Balsamic Dressing; toss well to coat. Arrange tomatoes, cut sides up, on a jelly-roll pan coated with cooking spray. Bake at 350° for 30 minutes or until tomatoes soften. Cool completely.

3. Combine tomatoes, baby arugula, and onion in a large bowl. Drizzle with the remaining 2 tablespoons Maple-Balsamic Dressing; toss gently to coat. Sprinkle evenly with cheese and pepper.

Calories 47; Fat 2.3g (sat 0.6g, mono 1.3g, poly 0.3g); Protein 1.5g; Carb 6g; Fiber 0.9g; Chol 1mg; Iron 0.7mg; Sodium 97mg; Calc 54mg

Maple-Balsamic Dressing

This sweet, tangy dressing is ideal for peppery greens, such as arugula, or bitter greens like radicchio or endive. It also complements rich meats, such as pork or dark-meat chicken.

Yield: About 1 cup (serving size: 1 tablespoon dressing)

½ cup tomato juice

⅓ cup balsamic vinegar

¼ cup maple syrup

1 tablespoon minced fresh rosemary

2 teaspoons Dijon mustard

½ teaspoon salt

½ teaspoon freshly ground black pepper

2 garlic cloves, minced

2½ tablespoons extra-virgin olive oil

1. Combine all ingredients except oil, stirring well. Gradually add oil, stirring constantly with a whisk until well combined.

2. Refrigerate dressing in an airtight container for up to five days; stir well before using.

Calories 39; Fat 2.3g (sat 0.3g, mono 1.7g, poly 0.2g); Protein 0.2g; Carb 4.7g; Fiber 0.1g; Chol 0mg; Iron 0.2mg; Sodium 118mg; Calc 8mg

Nutritional Analysis

How to Use It and Why

Glance at the end of any *Cooking Light* recipe, and you'll see how committed we are to helping you make the best of today's light cooking. With chefs, registered dietitians, home economists, and a computer system that analyzes every ingredient we use, *Cooking Light* gives you authoritative dietary detail like no other magazine. We go to such lengths so you can see how our recipes fit into your healthful eating plan. If you're trying to lose weight, the calorie and fat figures will probably help most. But if you're keeping a close eye on the sodium, cholesterol, and saturated fat in your diet, we provide those numbers, too. And because many women don't get enough iron or calcium, we can help there, as well. Finally, there's a fiber analysis for those of us who don't get enough roughage.

Here's a helpful guide to put our nutritional analysis numbers into perspective. Remember, one size doesn't fit all, so take your lifestyle, age, and circumstances into consideration when determining your nutrition needs. For example, pregnant or breast-feeding women need more protein, calories, and calcium. And women older than 50 need 1,200mg of calcium daily, 200mg more than the amount recommended for younger women.

In Our Nutritional Analysis, We Use These Abbreviations

sat saturated fat		**CHOL** cholesterol	
mono monounsaturated fat		**CALC** calcium	
poly polyunsaturated fat		**g** gram	
CARB carbohydrates		**mg** milligram	

Daily Nutrition Guide

	Women ages 25 to 50	Women over 50	Men ages 24 to 50	Men over 50
Calories	2,000	2,000 or less	2,700	2,500
Protein	50g	50g or less	63g	60g
Fat	65g or less	65g or less	88g or less	83g or less
Saturated Fat	20g or less	20g or less	27g or less	25g or less
Carbohydrates	304g	304g	410g	375g
Fiber	25g to 35g	25g to 35g	25g to 35g	25g to 35g
Cholesterol	300mg or less	300mg or less	300mg or less	300mg or less
Iron	18mg	8mg	8mg	8mg
Sodium	2,300mg or less	1,500mg or less	2,300mg or less	1,500mg or less
Calcium	1,000mg	1,200mg	1,000mg	1,000mg

The nutritional values used in our calculations either come from The Food Processor, Version 8.9 (ESHA Research), or are provided by food manufacturers.

Metric Equivalents

The information in the following charts is provided to help cooks outside the United States successfully use the recipes in this book. All equivalents are approximate.

Cooking/Oven Temperatures

	Fahrenheit	Celsius	Gas Mark
Freeze Water	32° F	0° C	
Room Temp.	68° F	20° C	
Boil Water	212° F	100° C	
Bake	325° F	160° C	3
	350° F	180° C	4
	375° F	190° C	5
	400° F	200° C	6
	425° F	220° C	7
	450° F	230° C	8
Broil			Grill

Liquid Ingredients by Volume

¼ tsp	=					1 ml	
½ tsp	=					2 ml	
1 tsp	=					5 ml	
3 tsp	=	1 tbl	=	½ fl oz	=	15 ml	
2 tbls	=	⅛ cup	=	1 fl oz	=	30 ml	
4 tbls	=	¼ cup	=	2 fl oz	=	60 ml	
5⅓ tbls	=	⅓ cup	=	3 fl oz	=	80 ml	
8 tbls	=	½ cup	=	4 fl oz	=	120 ml	
10⅔ tbls	=	⅔ cup	=	5 fl oz	=	160 ml	
12 tbls	=	¾ cup	=	6 fl oz	=	180 ml	
16 tbls	=	1 cup	=	8 fl oz	=	240 ml	
1 pt	=	2 cups	=	16 fl oz	=	480 ml	
1 qt	=	4 cups	=	32 fl oz	=	960 ml	
				33 fl oz	=	1000 ml	= 1 l

Dry Ingredients by Weight

(To convert ounces to grams, multiply the number of ounces by 30.)

1 oz	=	¹⁄₁₆ lb	=	30 g
4 oz	=	¼ lb	=	120 g
8 oz	=	½ lb	=	240 g
12 oz	=	¾ lb	=	360 g
16 oz	=	1 lb	=	480 g

Length

(To convert inches to centimeters, multiply the number of inches by 2.5.)

1 in	=				2.5 cm	
6 in	=	½ ft		=	15 cm	
12 in	=	1 ft		=	30 cm	
36 in	=	3 ft	= 1 yd	=	90 cm	
40 in	=				100 cm	= 1 m

Equivalents for Different Types of Ingredients

Standard Cup	Fine Powder (ex. flour)	Grain (ex. rice)	Granular (ex. sugar)	Liquid Solids (ex. butter)	Liquid (ex. milk)
1	140 g	150 g	190 g	200 g	240 ml
¾	105 g	113 g	143 g	150 g	180 ml
⅔	93 g	100 g	125 g	133 g	160 ml
½	70 g	75 g	95 g	100 g	120 ml
⅓	47 g	50 g	63 g	67 g	80 ml
¼	35 g	38 g	48 g	50 g	60 ml
⅛	18 g	19 g	24 g	25 g	30 ml

Index